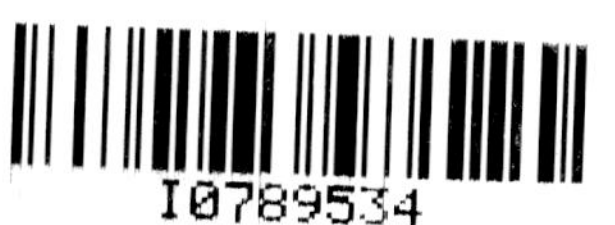

Amazing
SLOTH
Coloring Book For
GIRLS

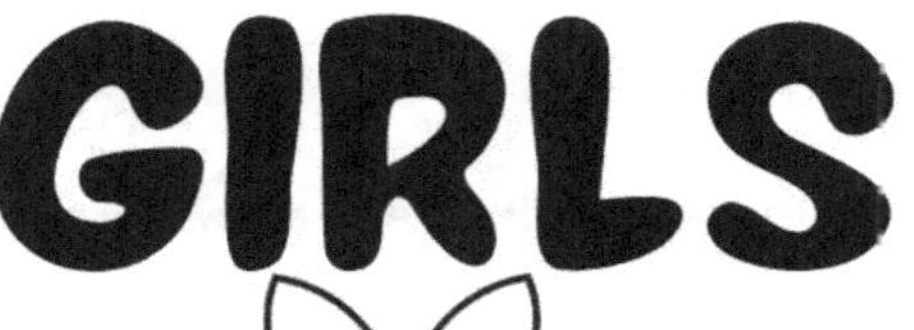

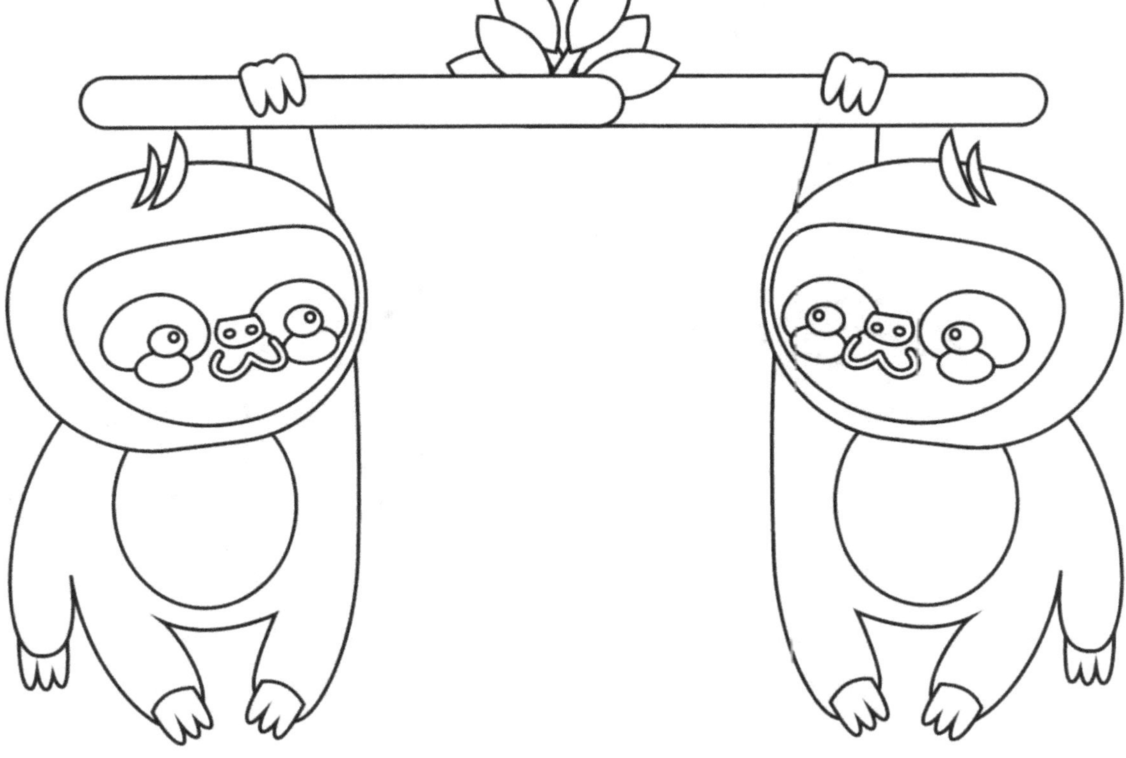

Sloth

This Book Belongs To

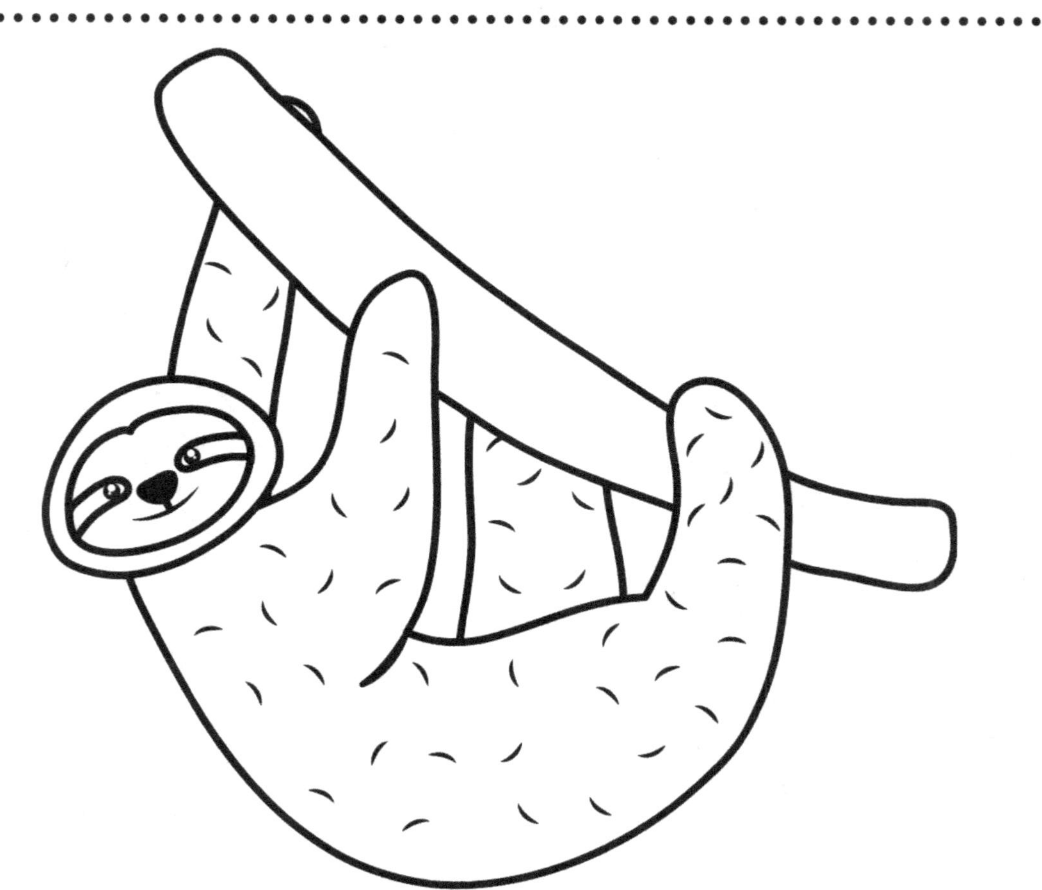

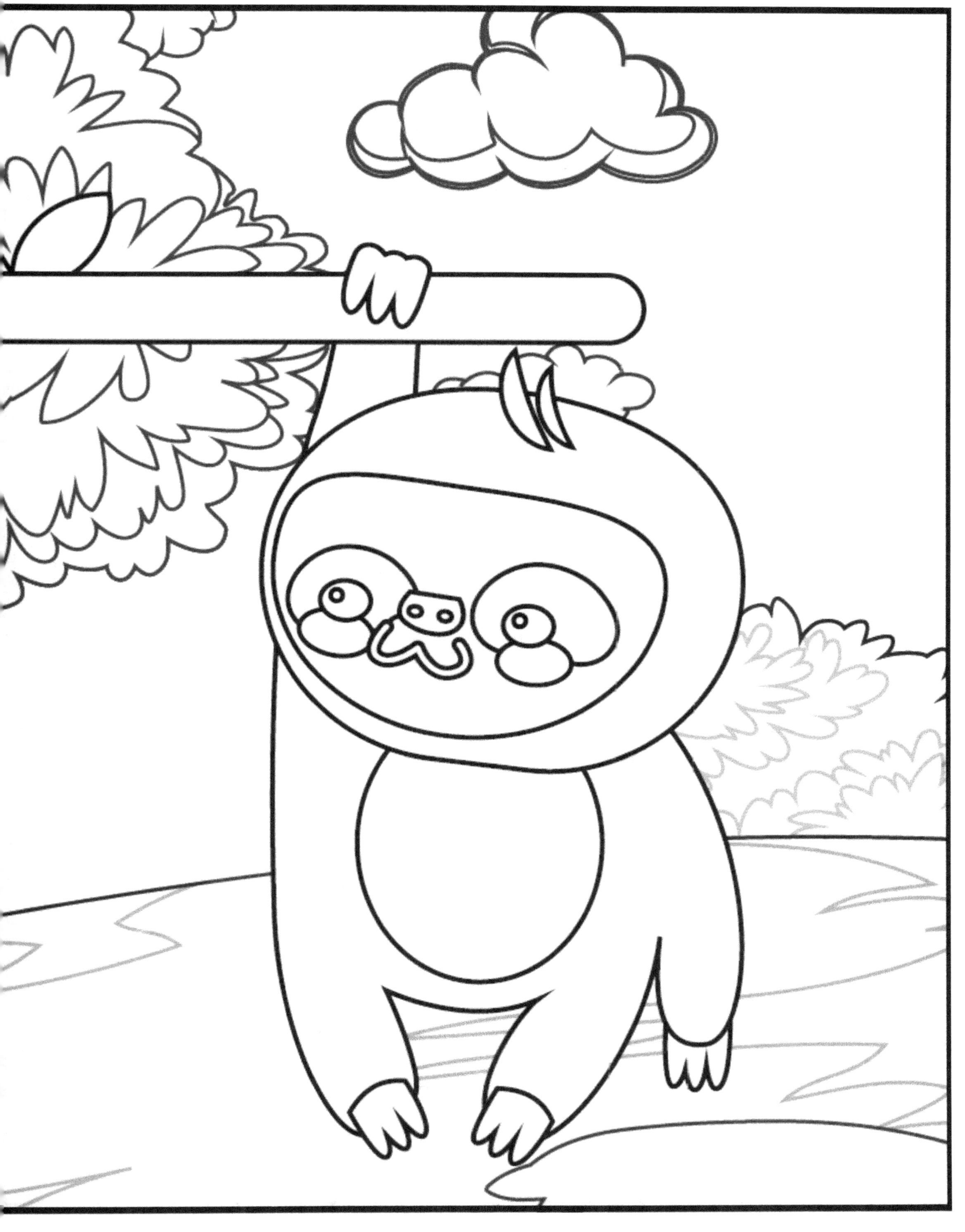

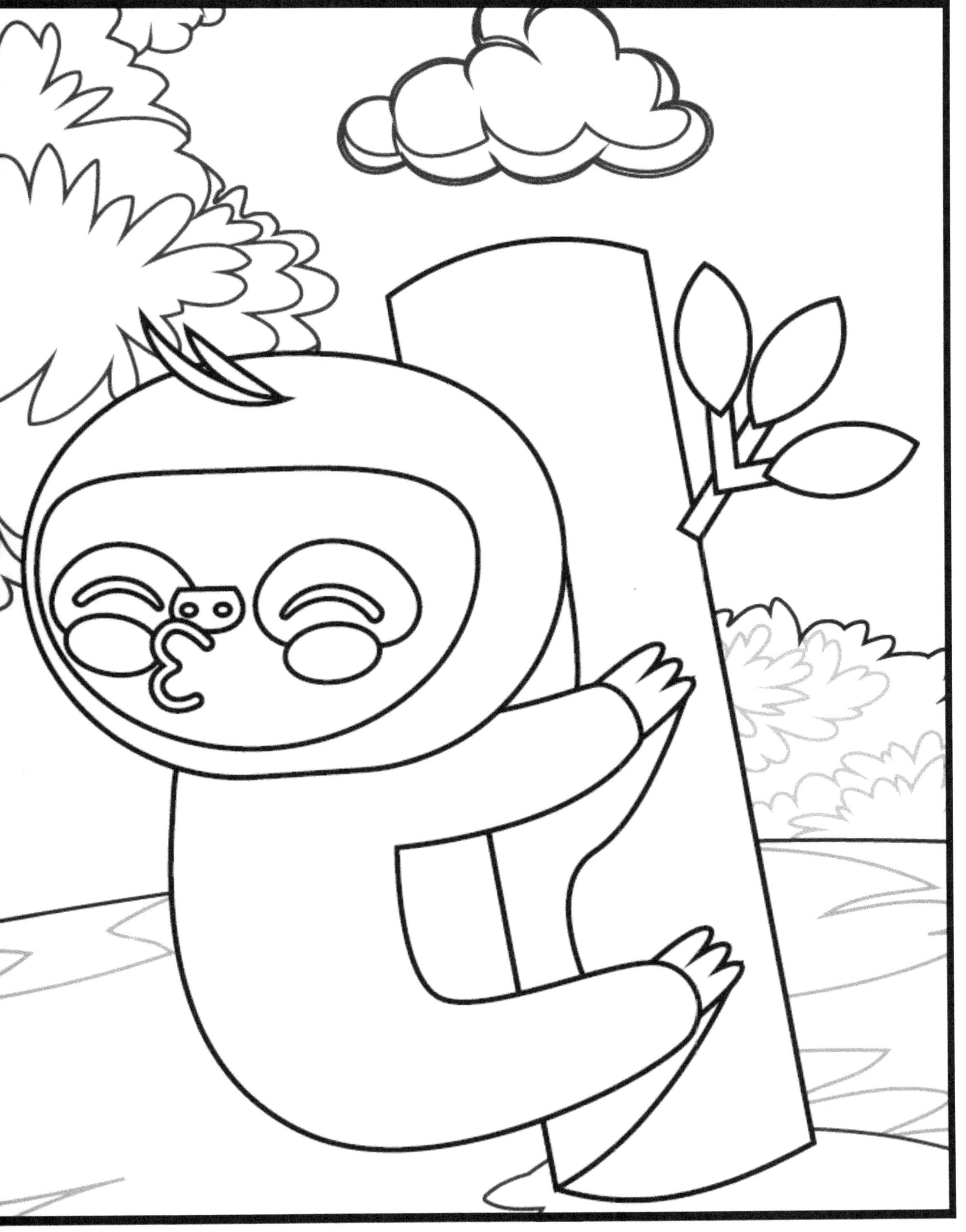

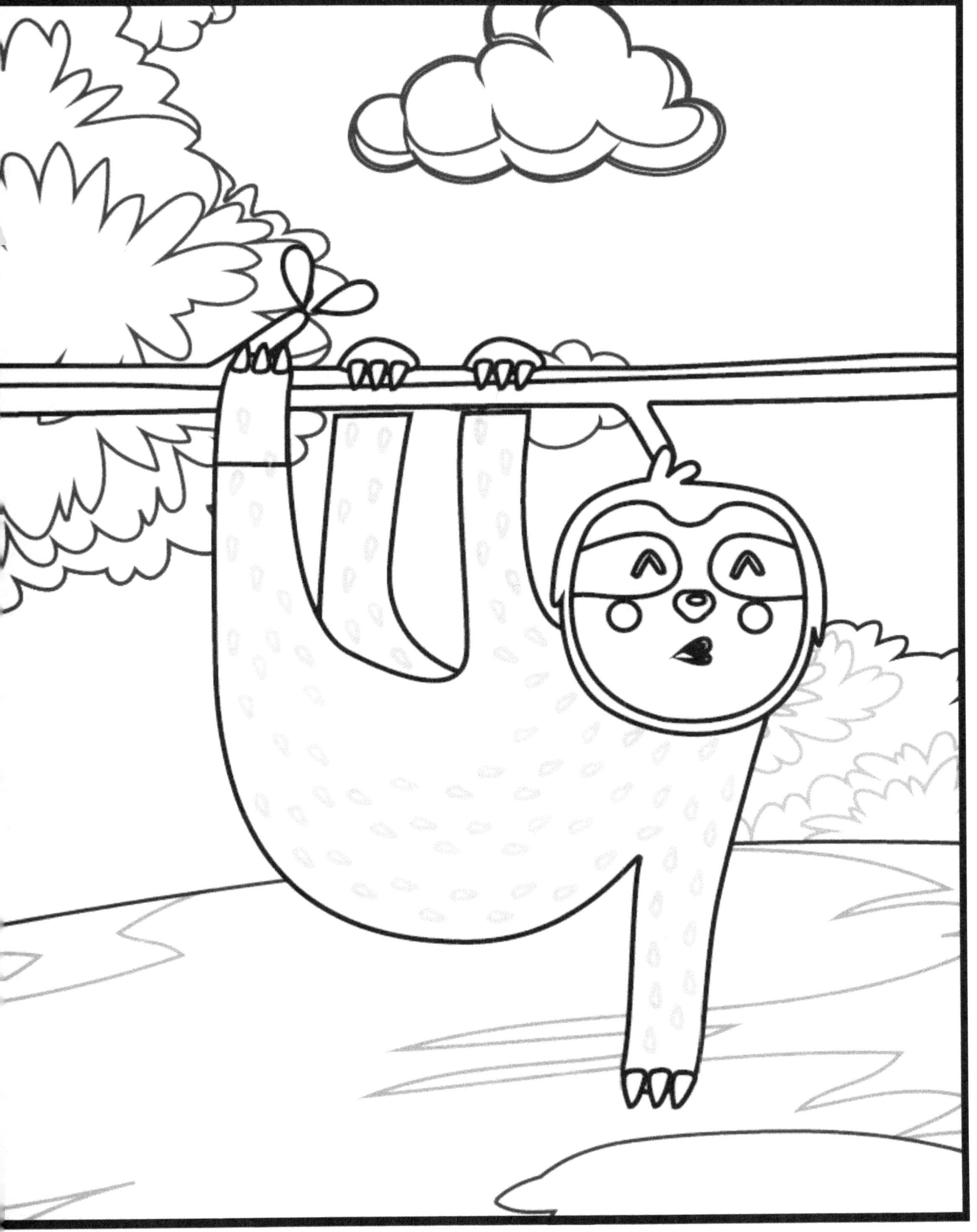

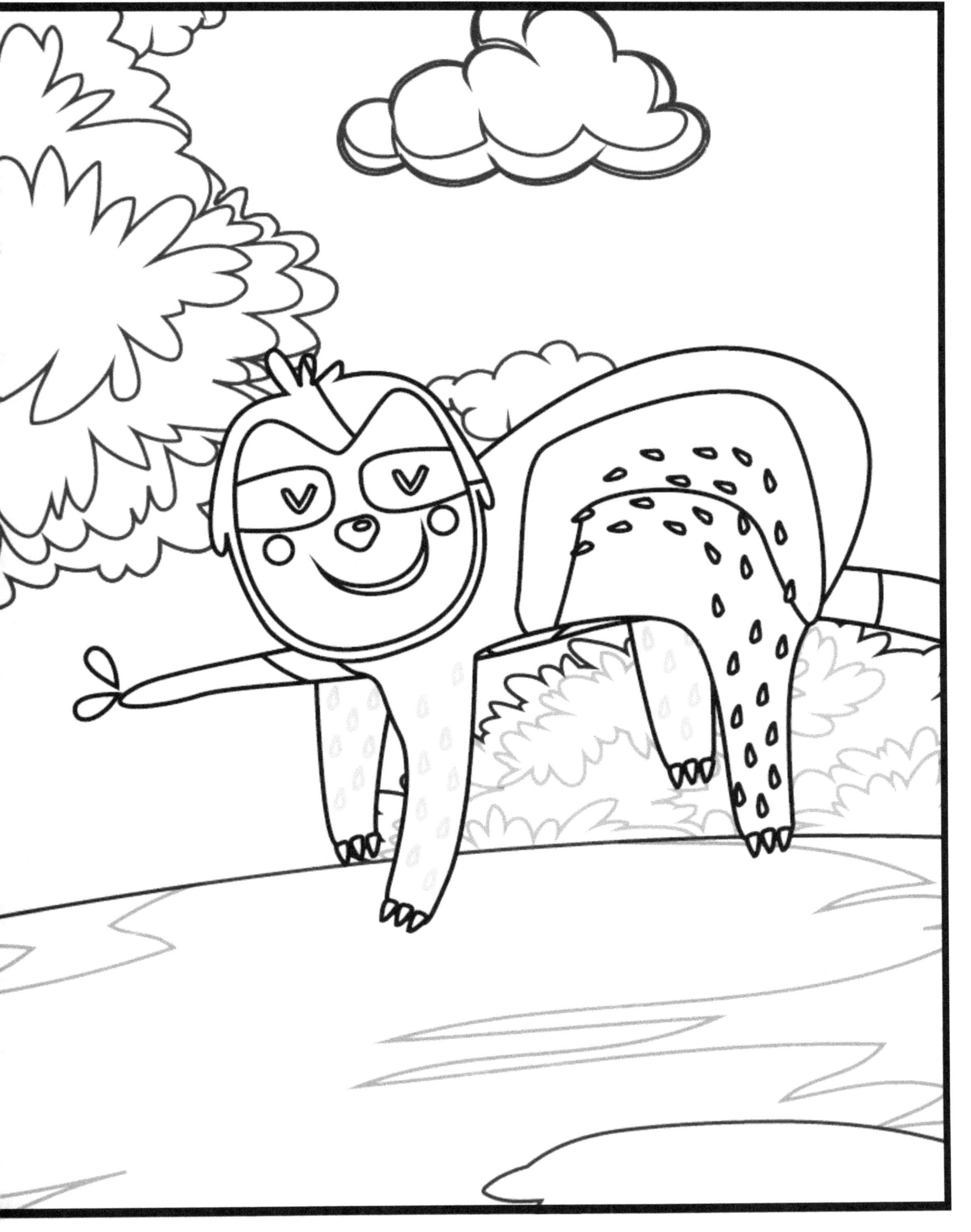

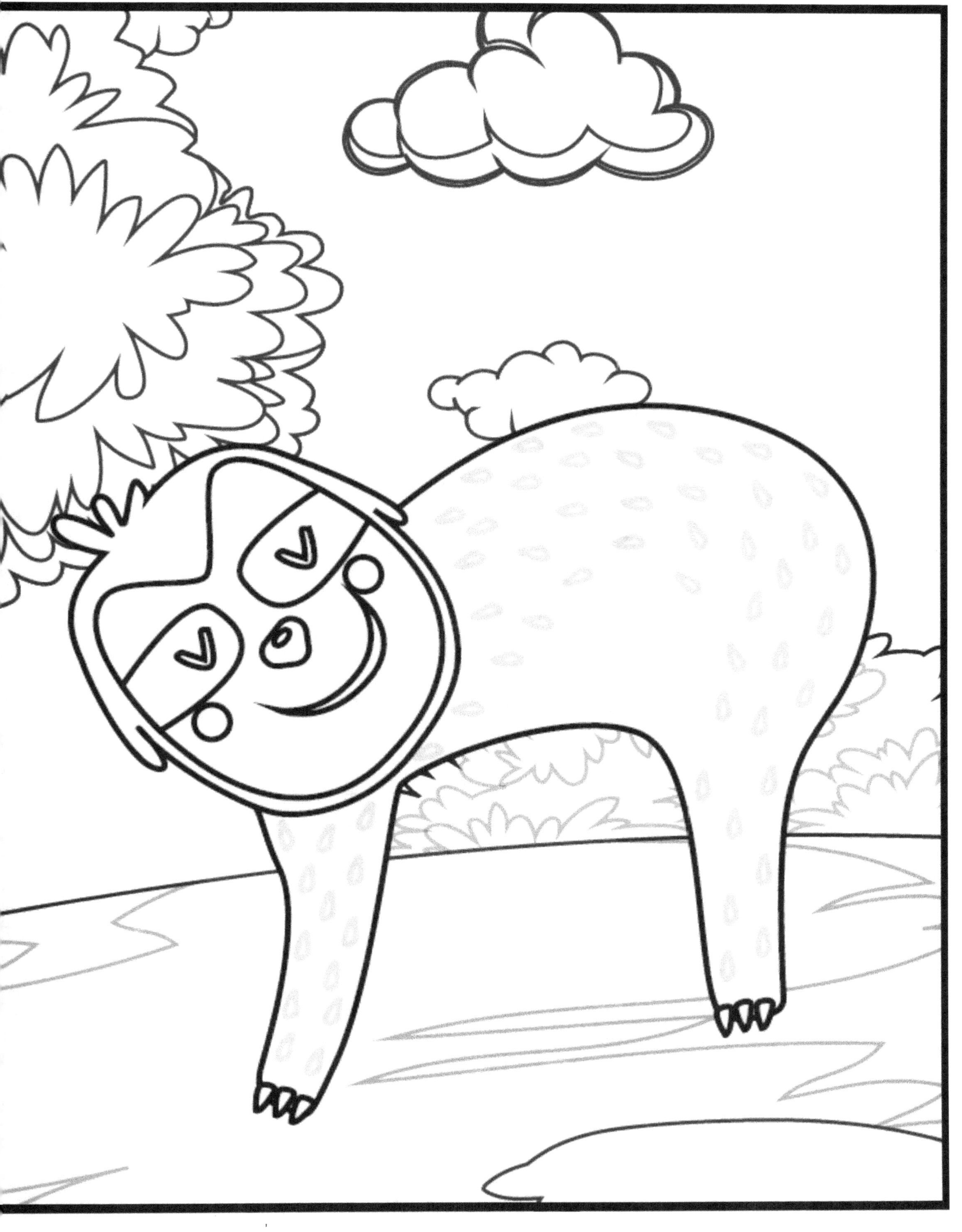

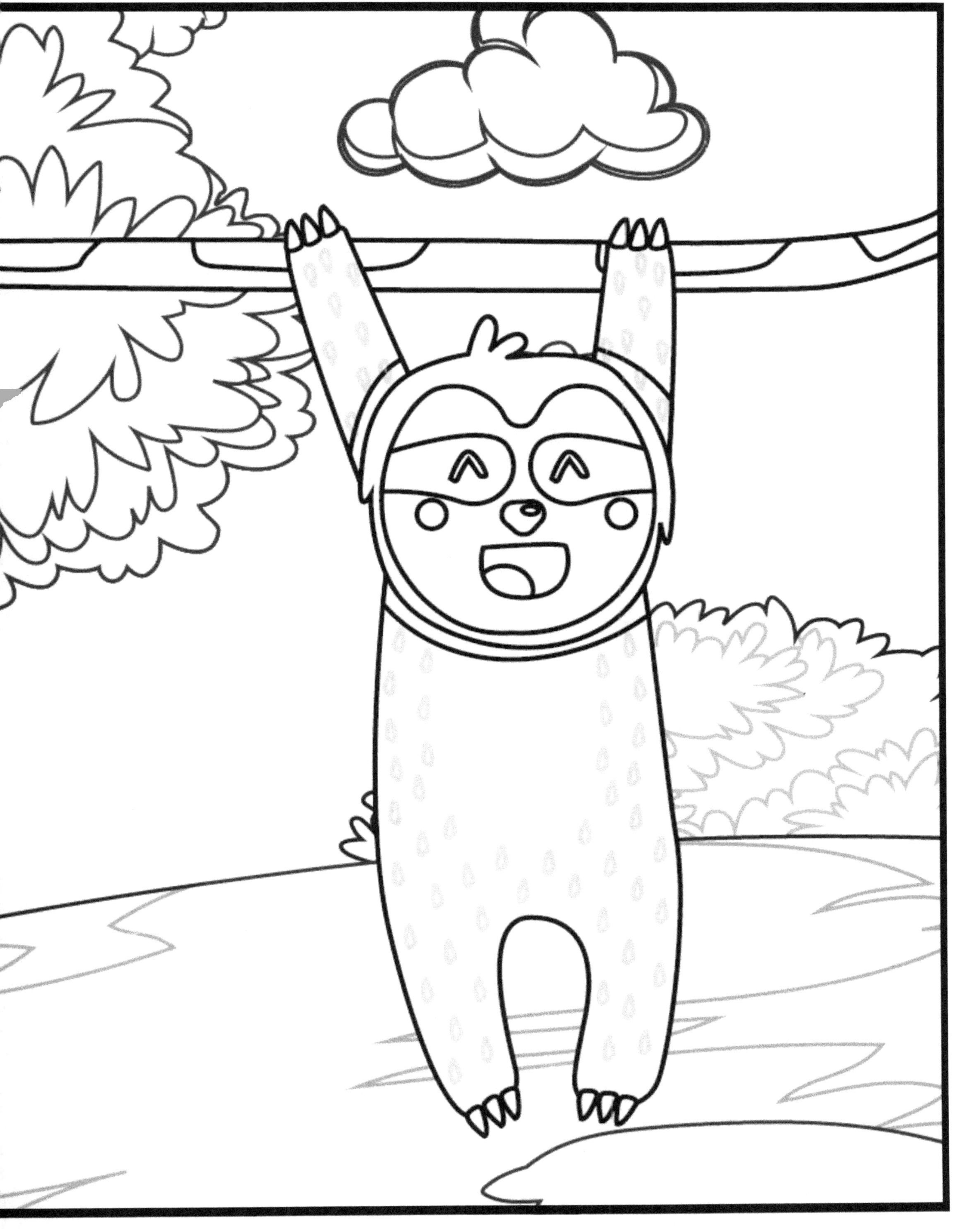

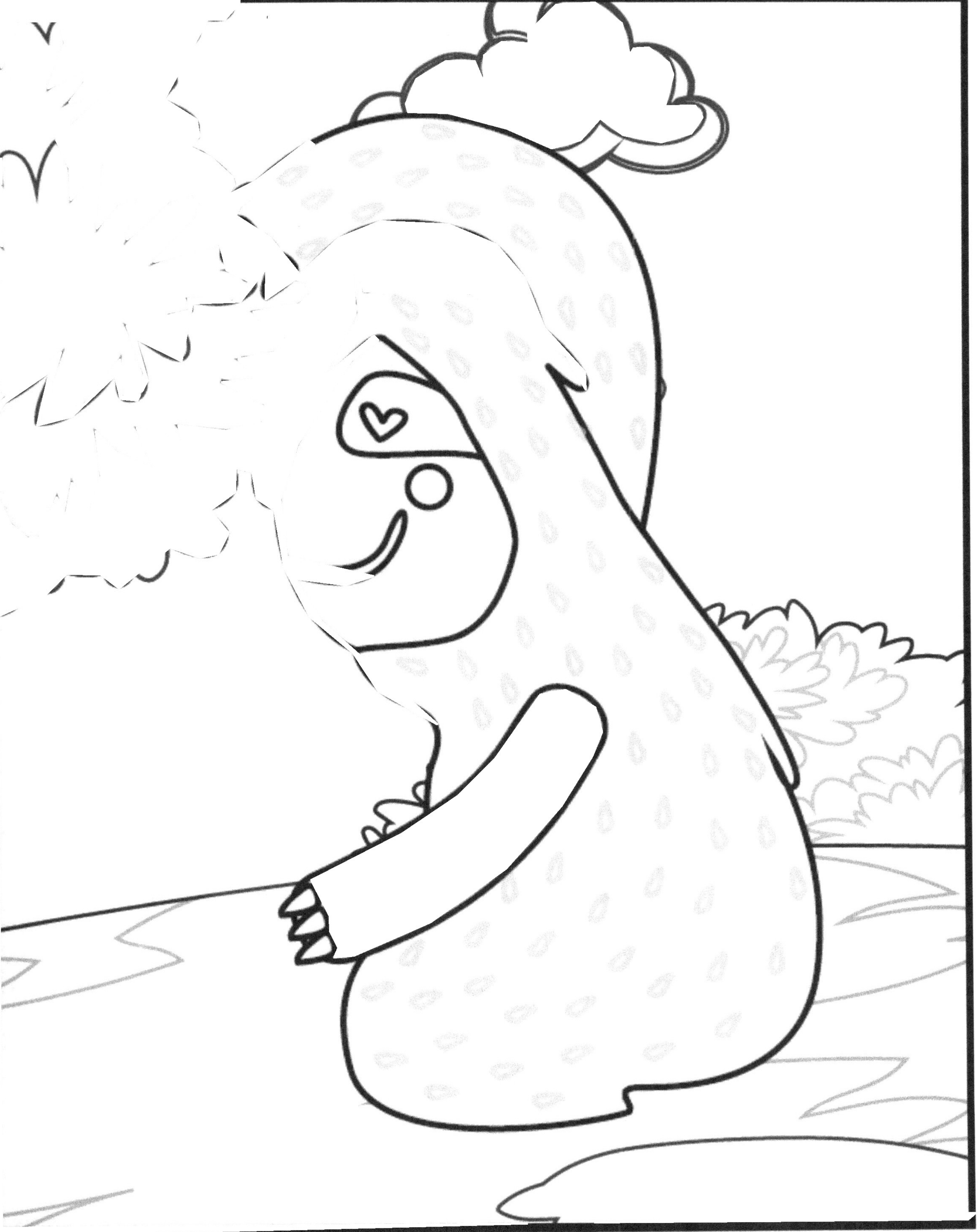

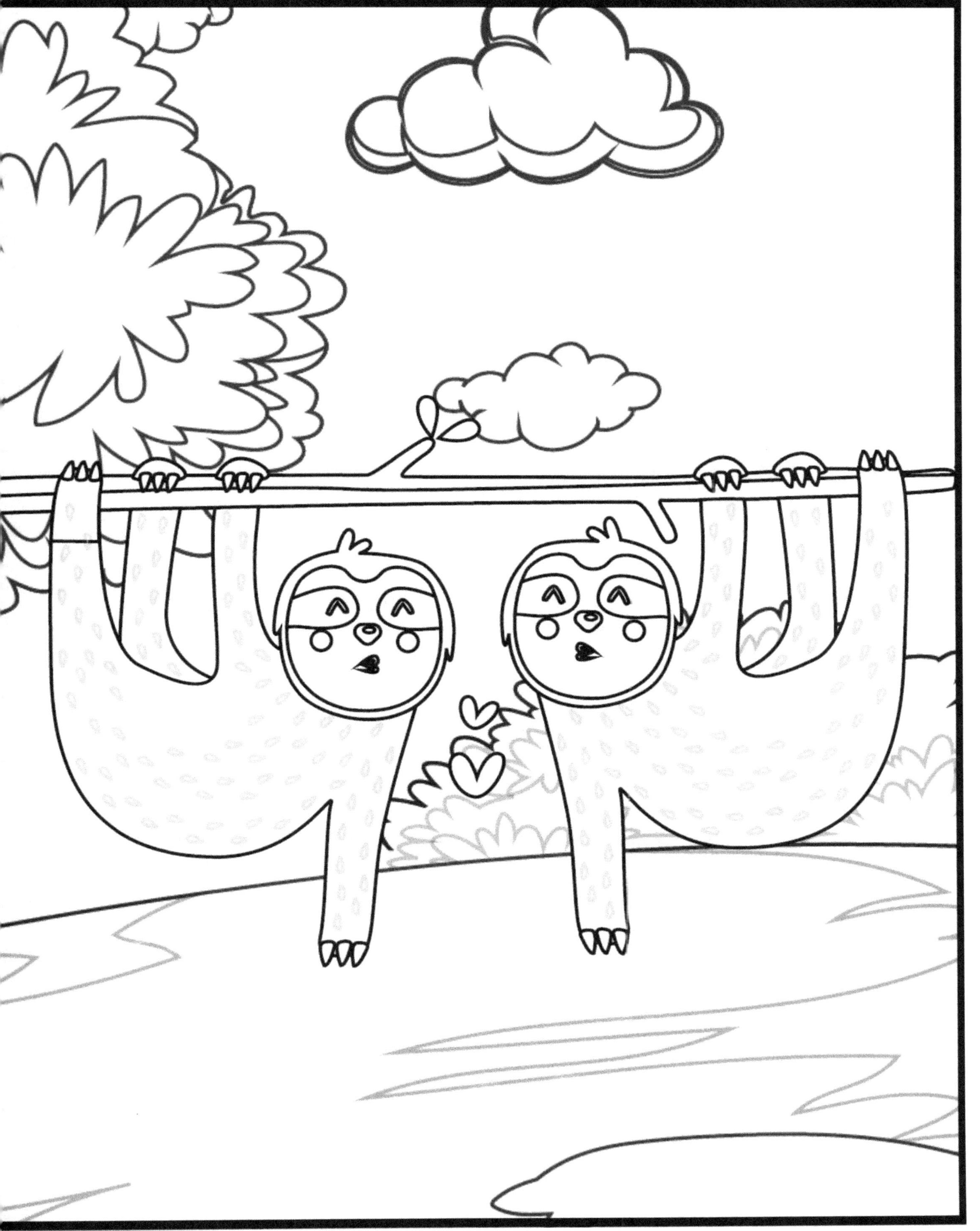

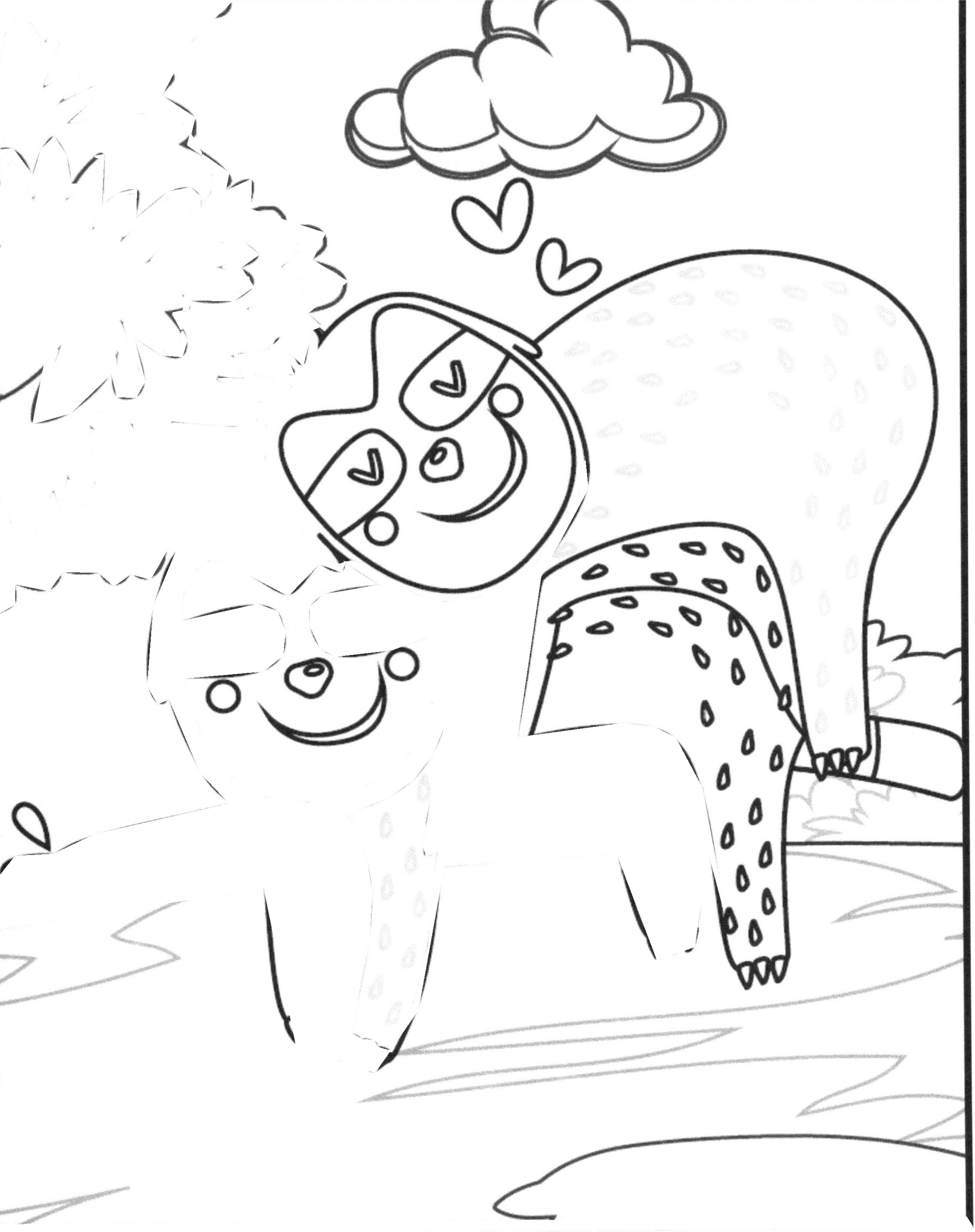

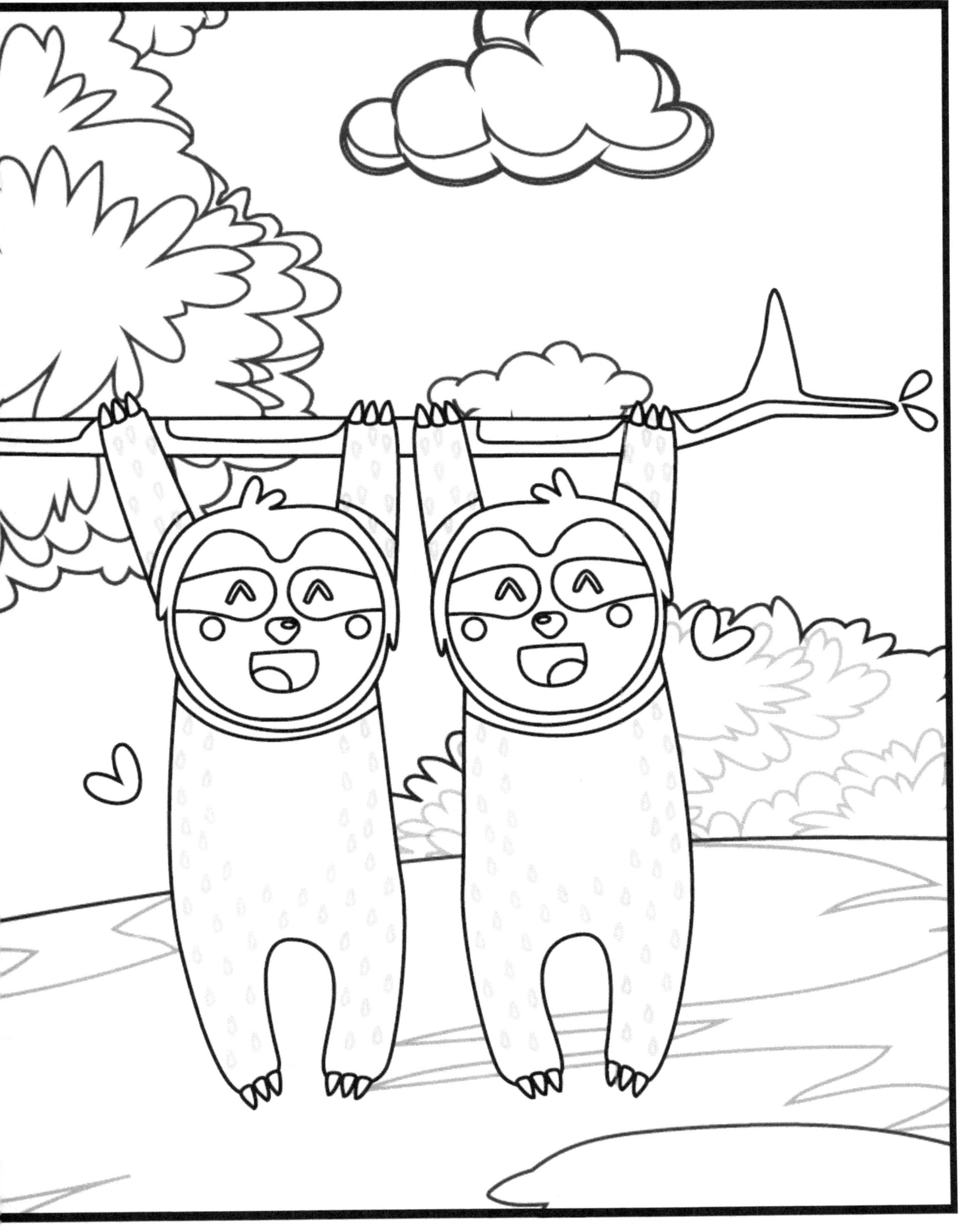

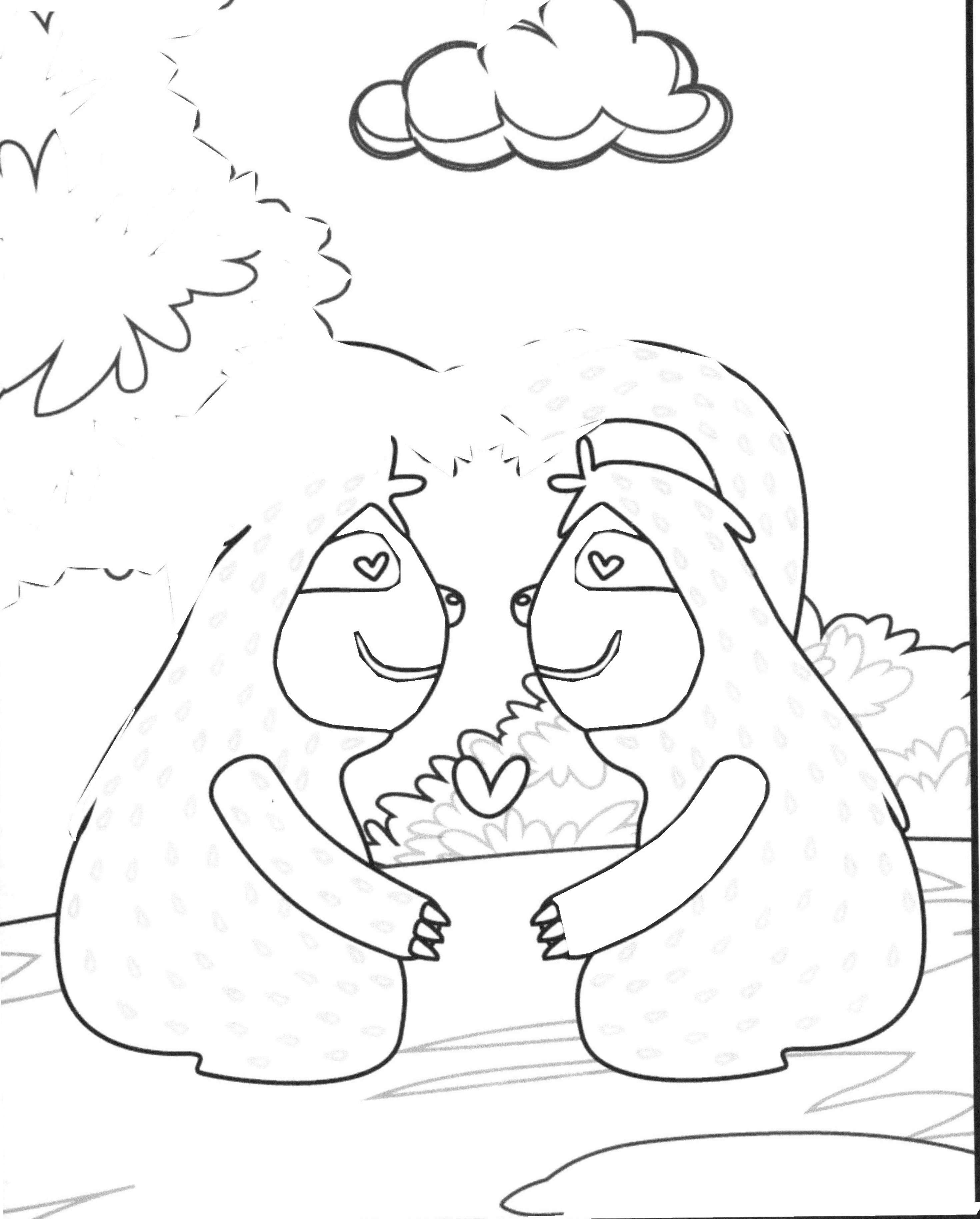

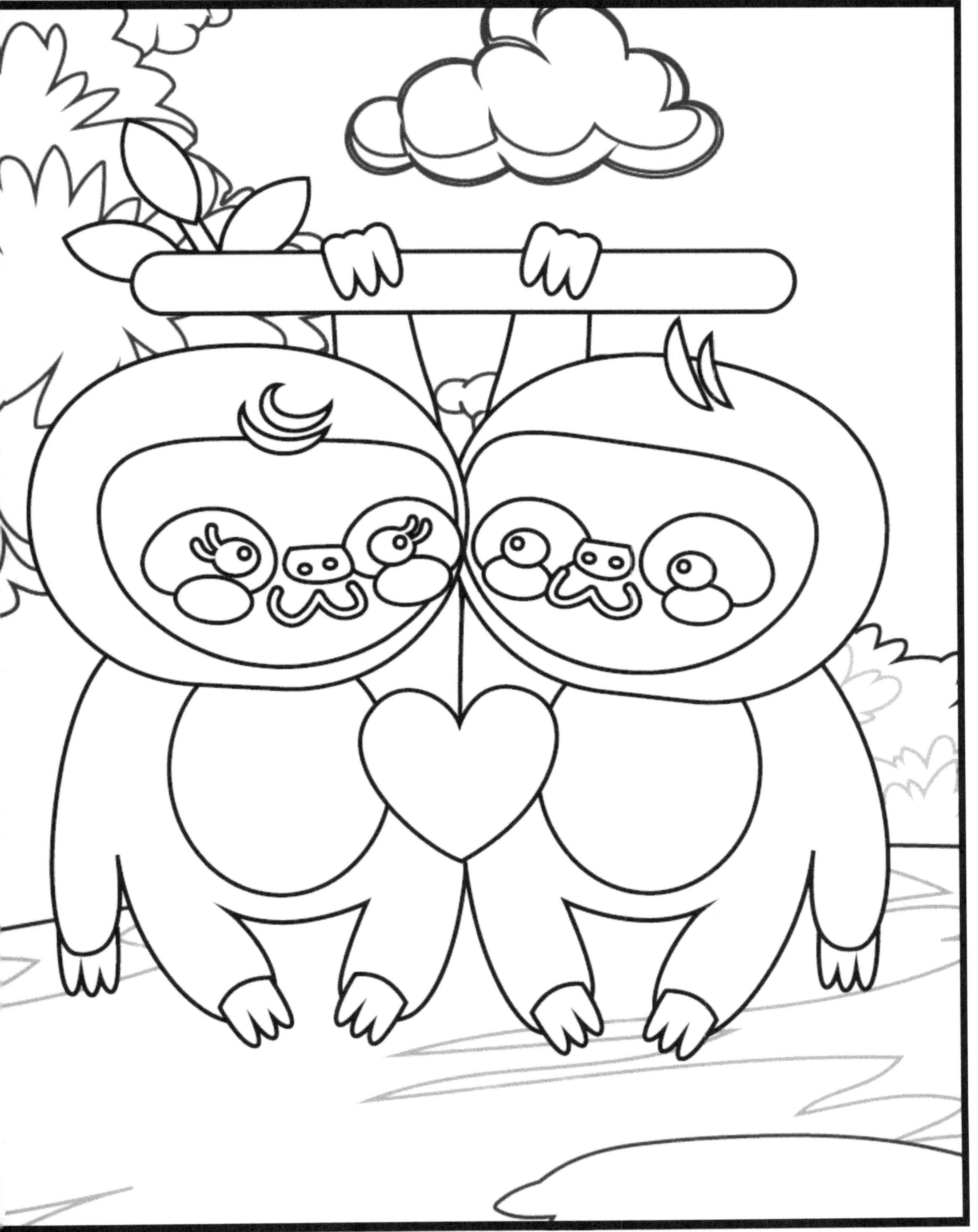

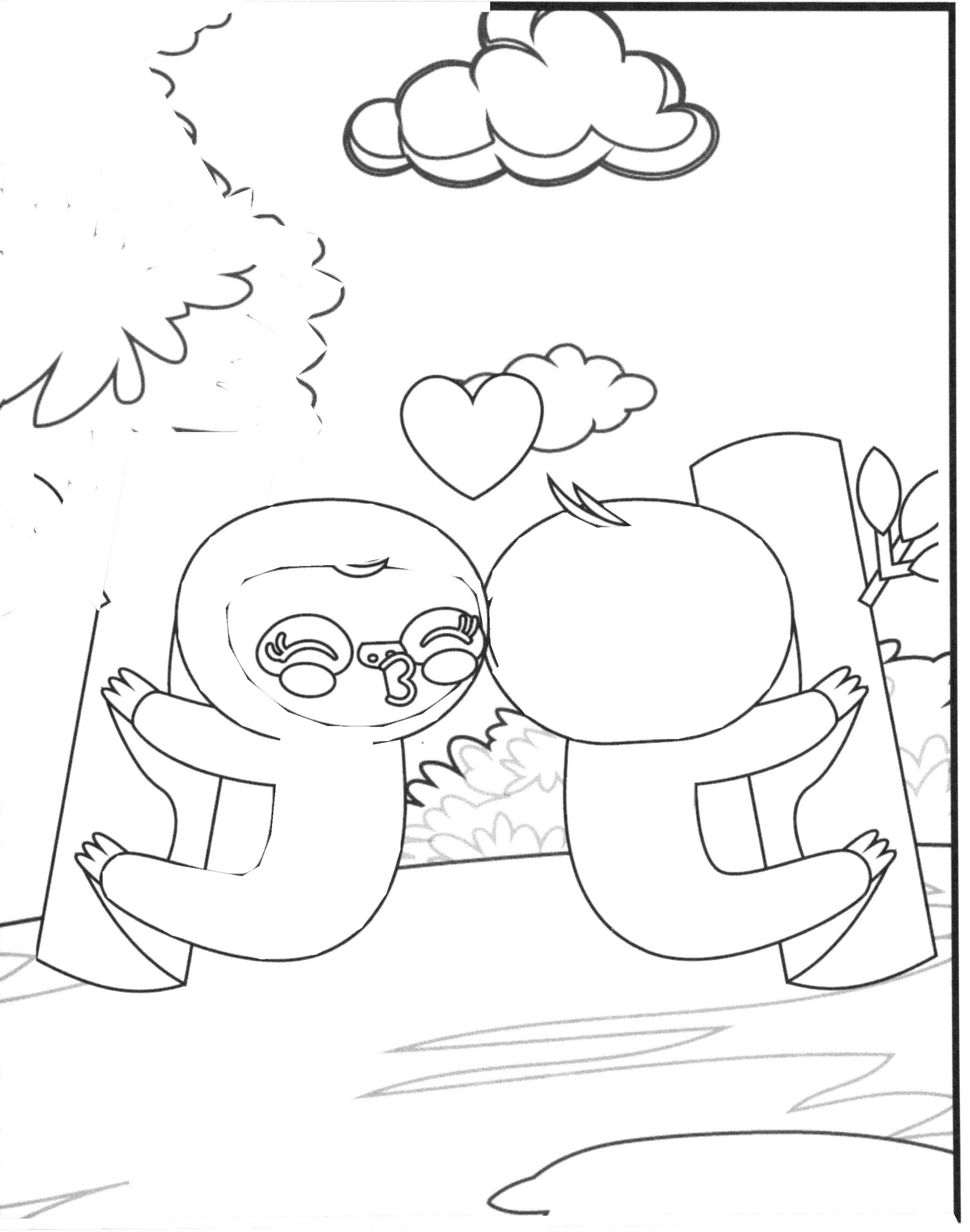

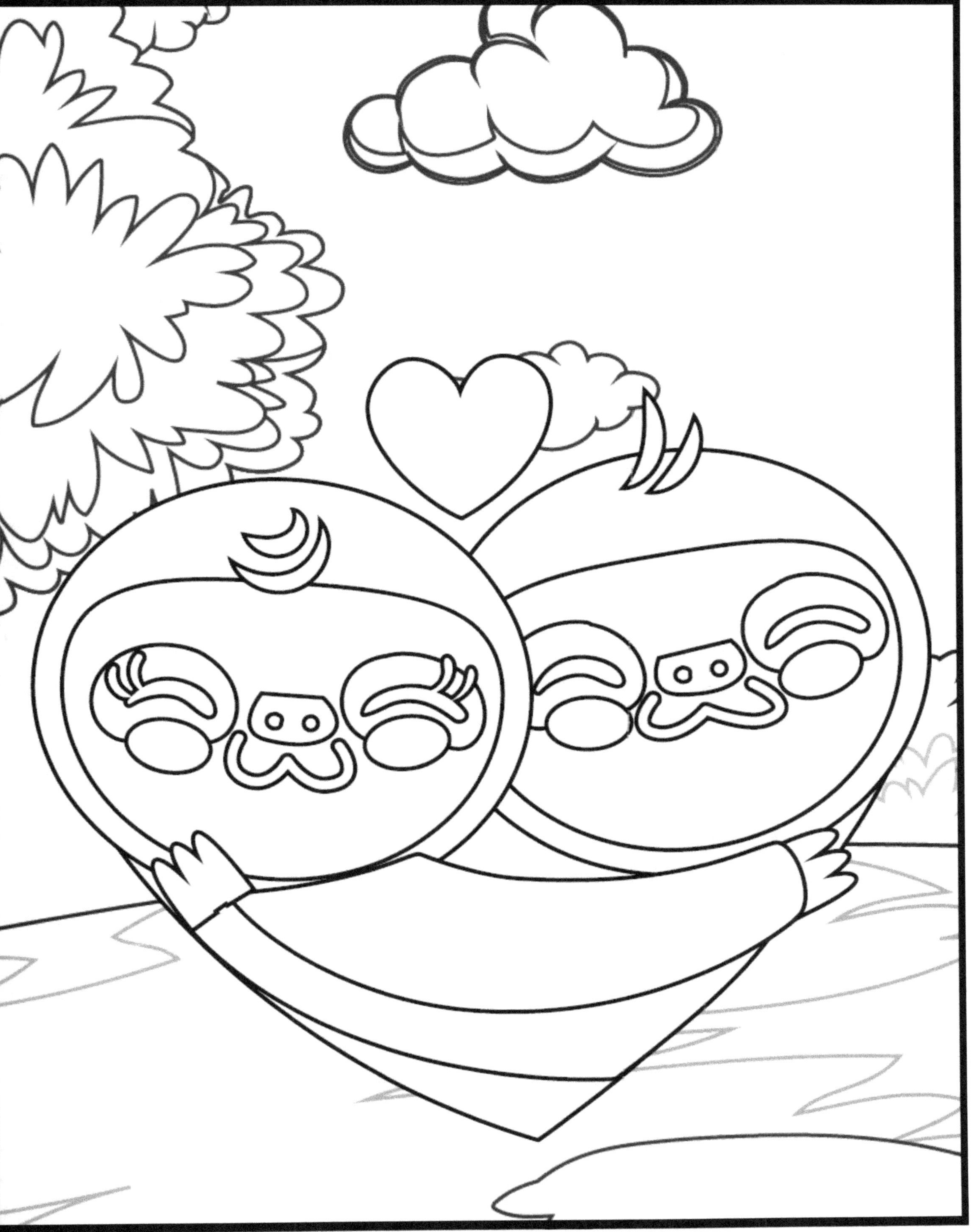

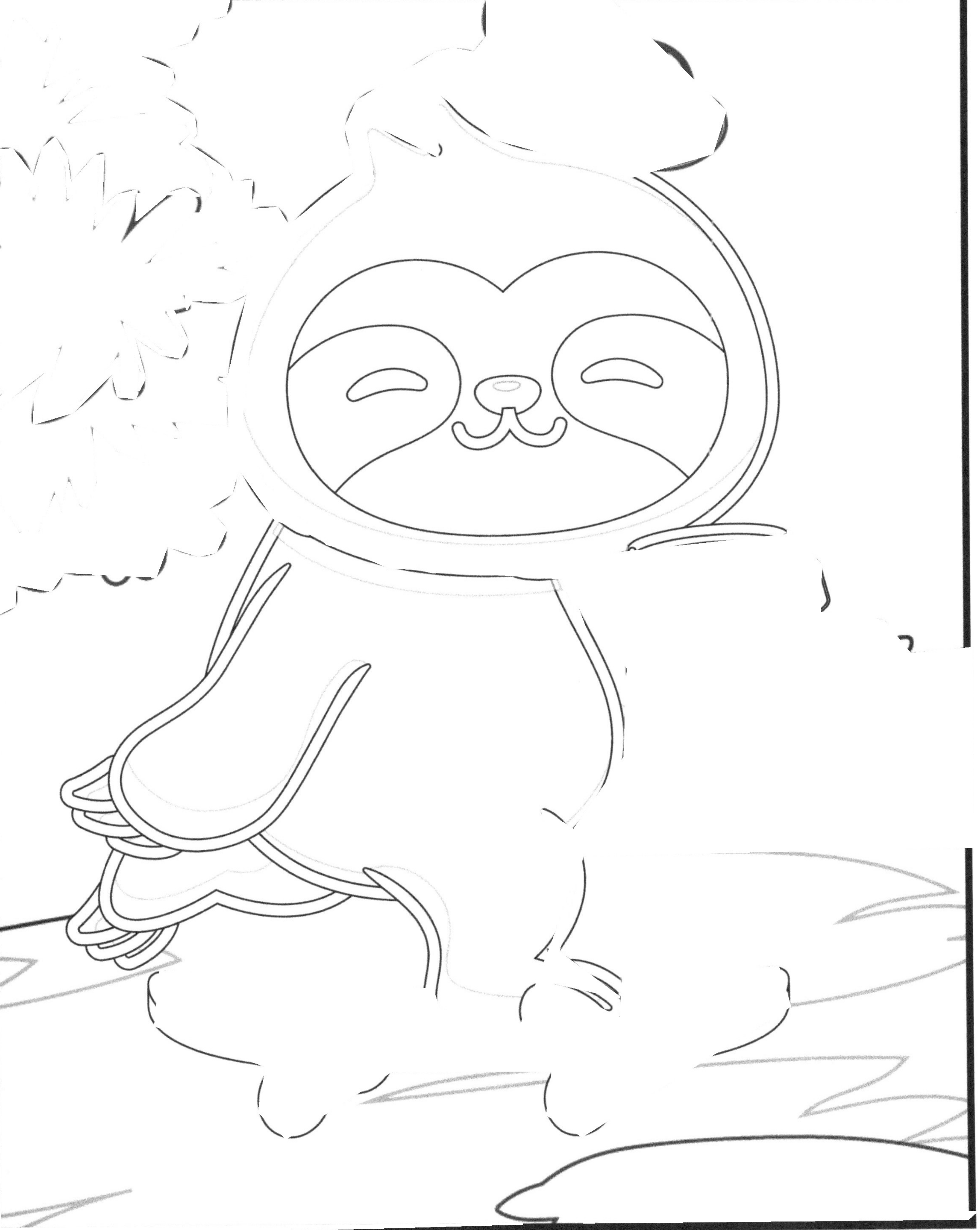

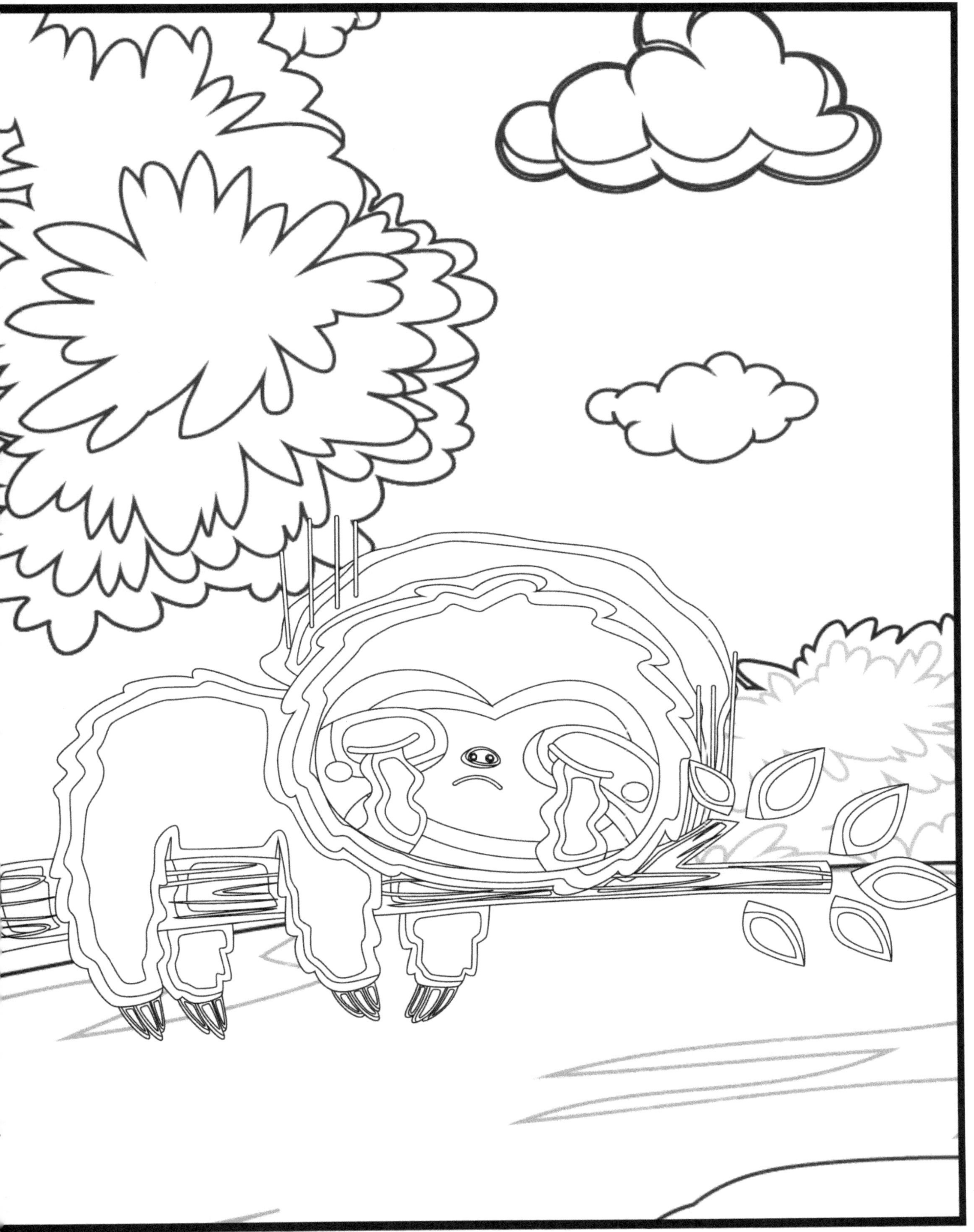

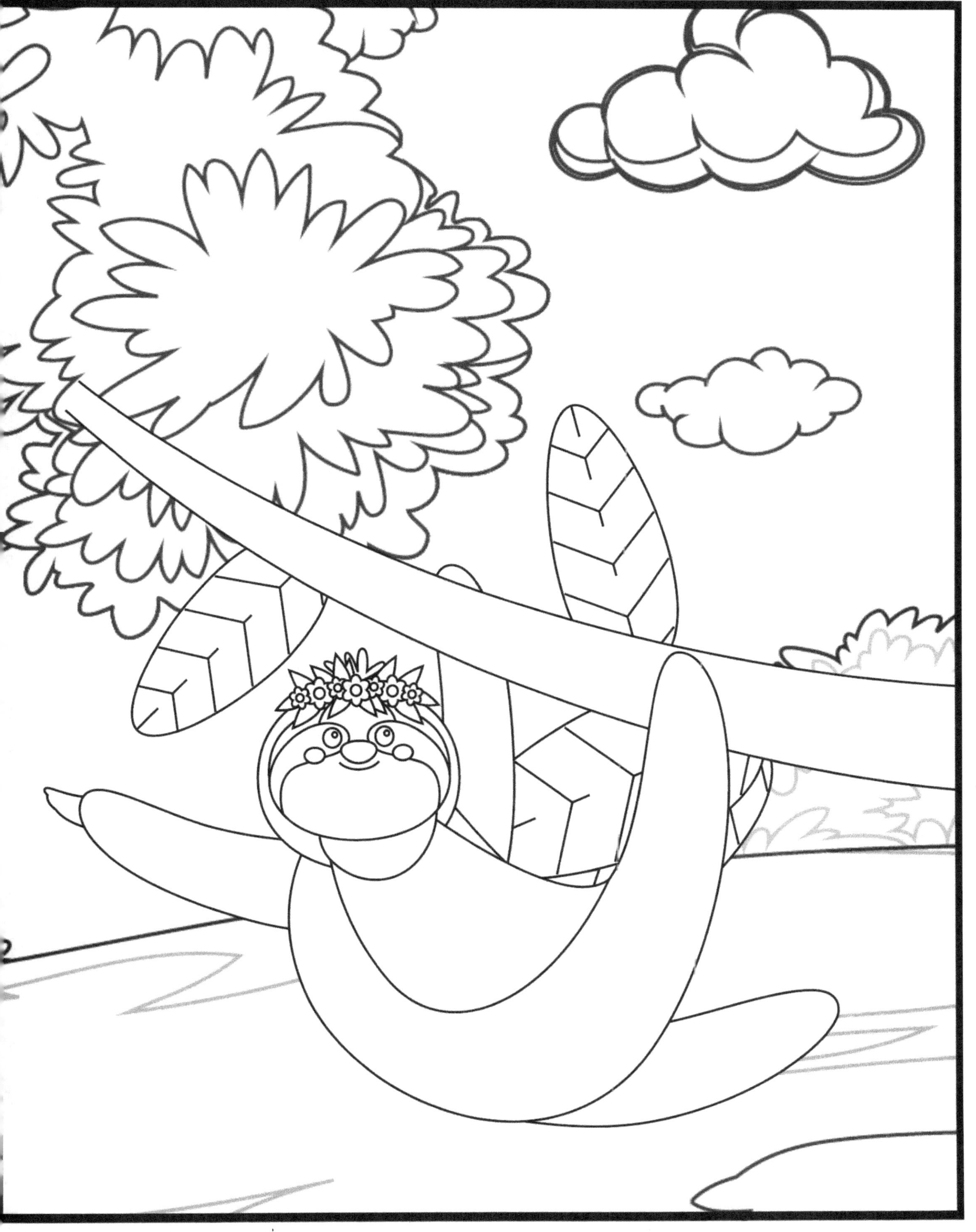

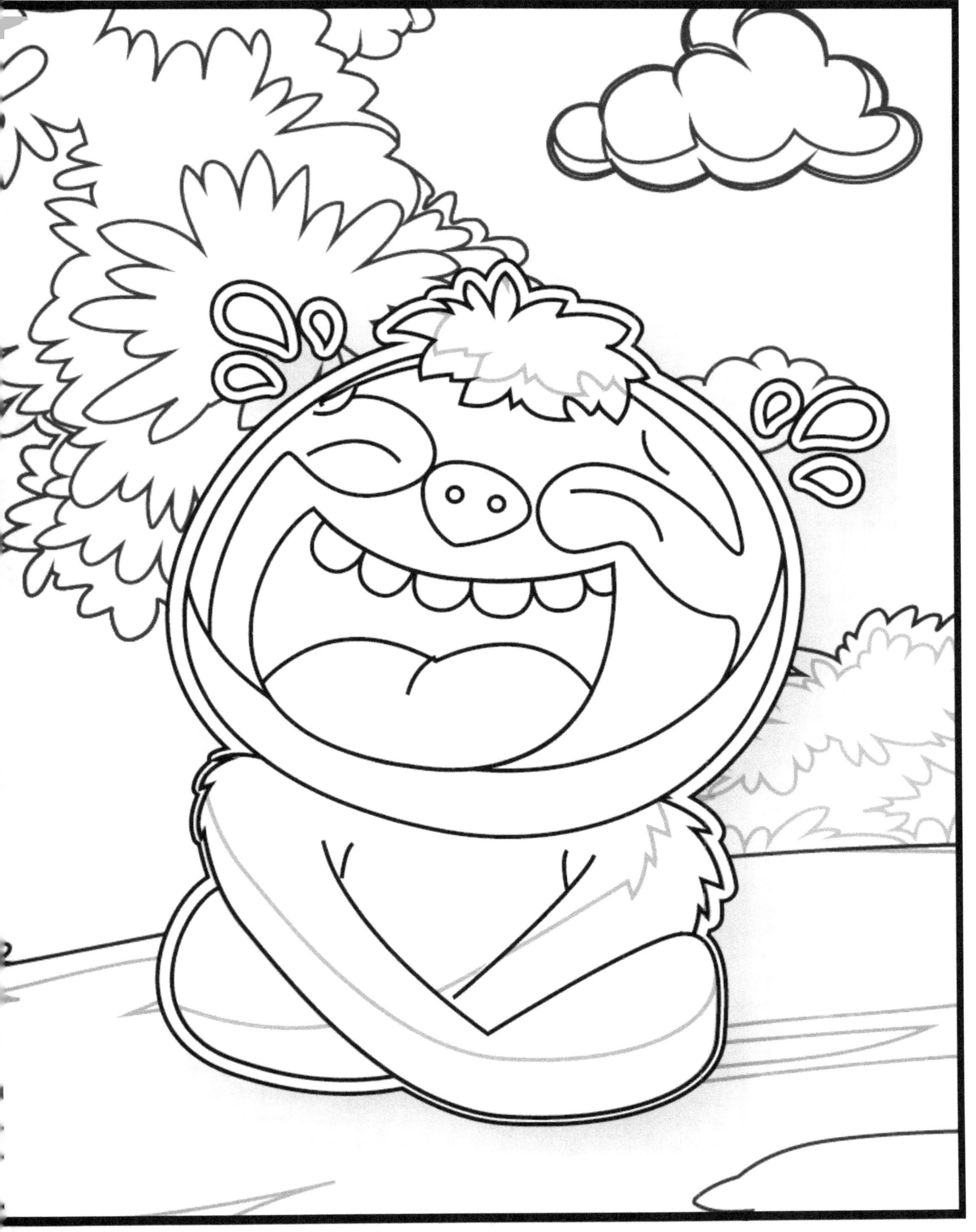

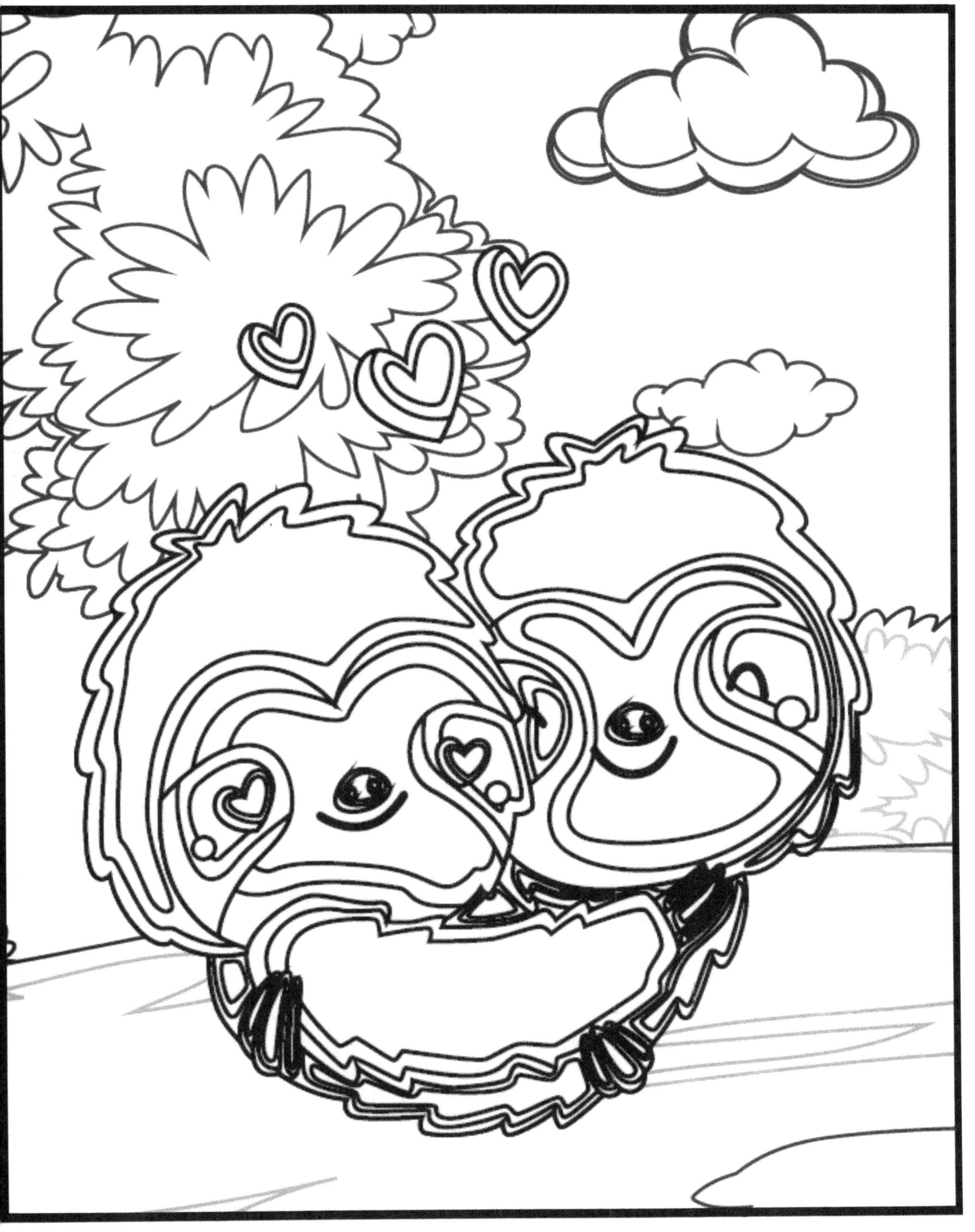

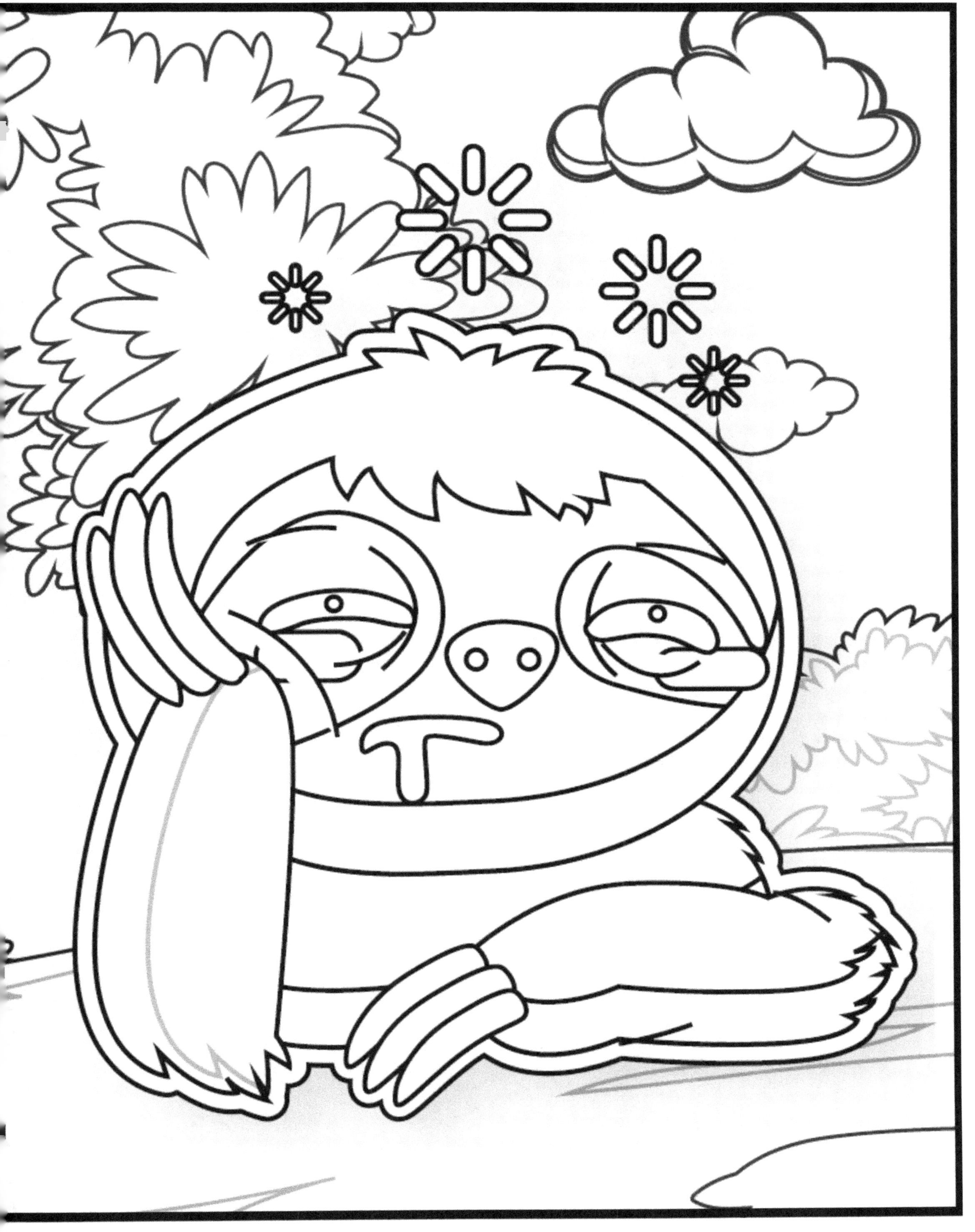

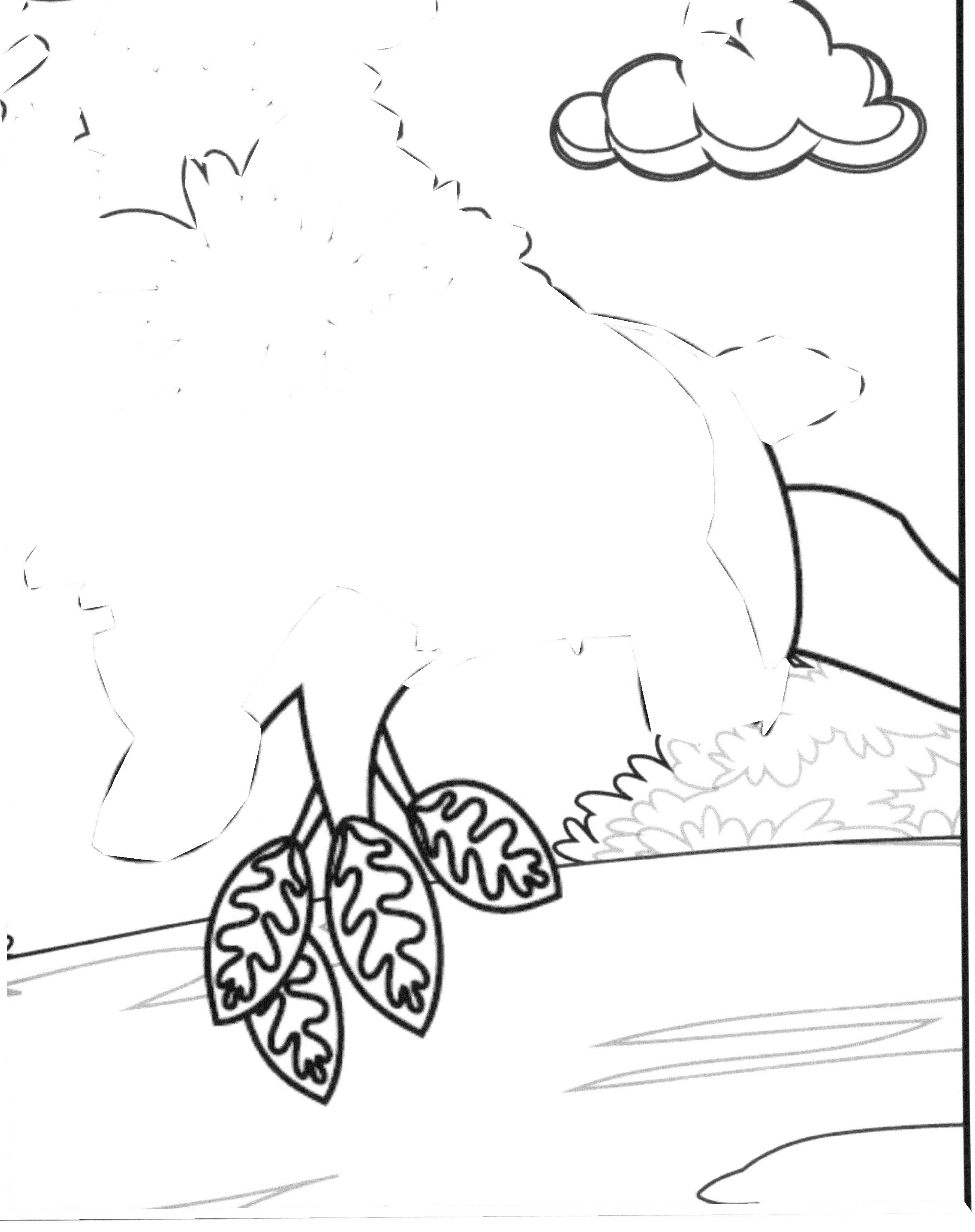

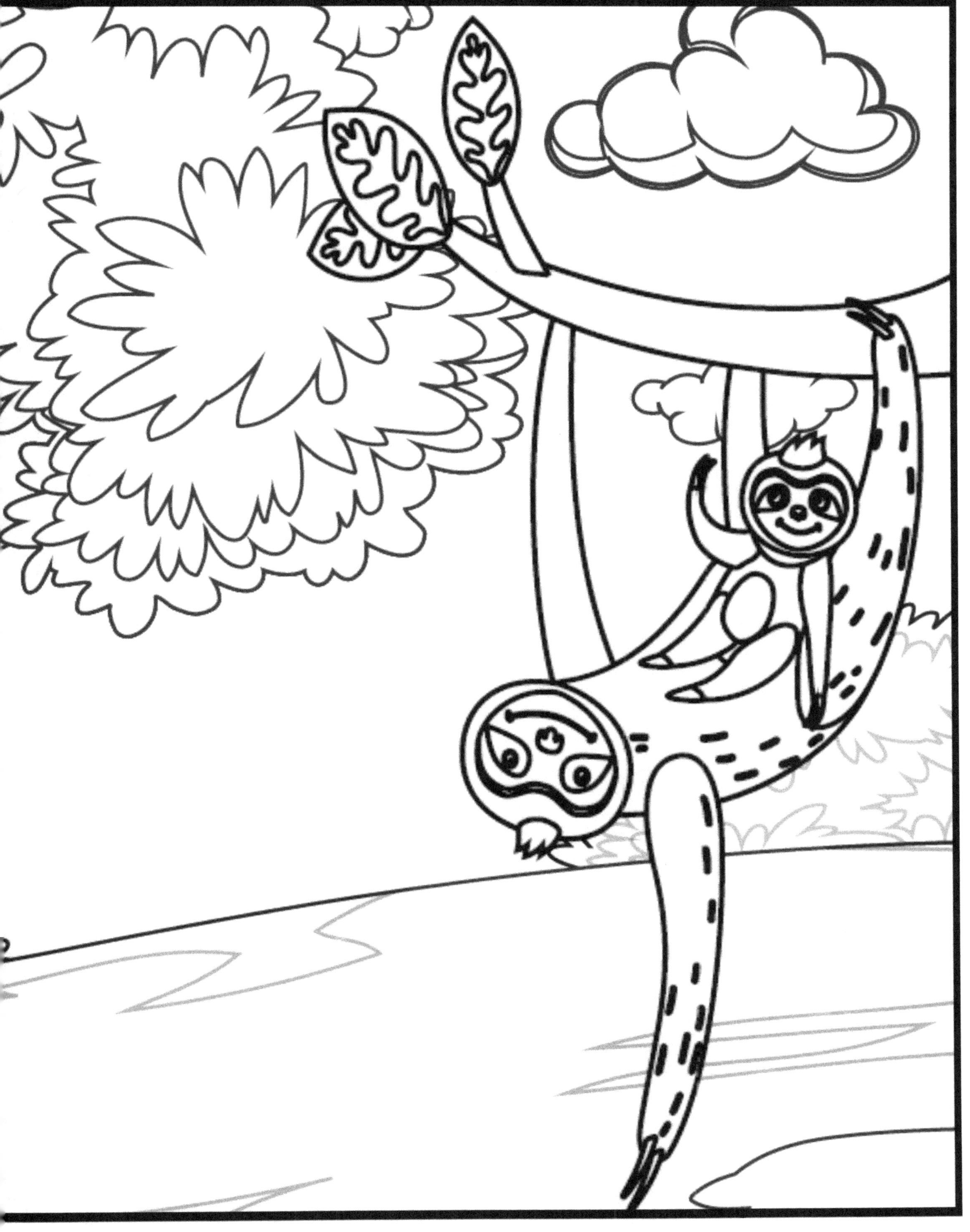

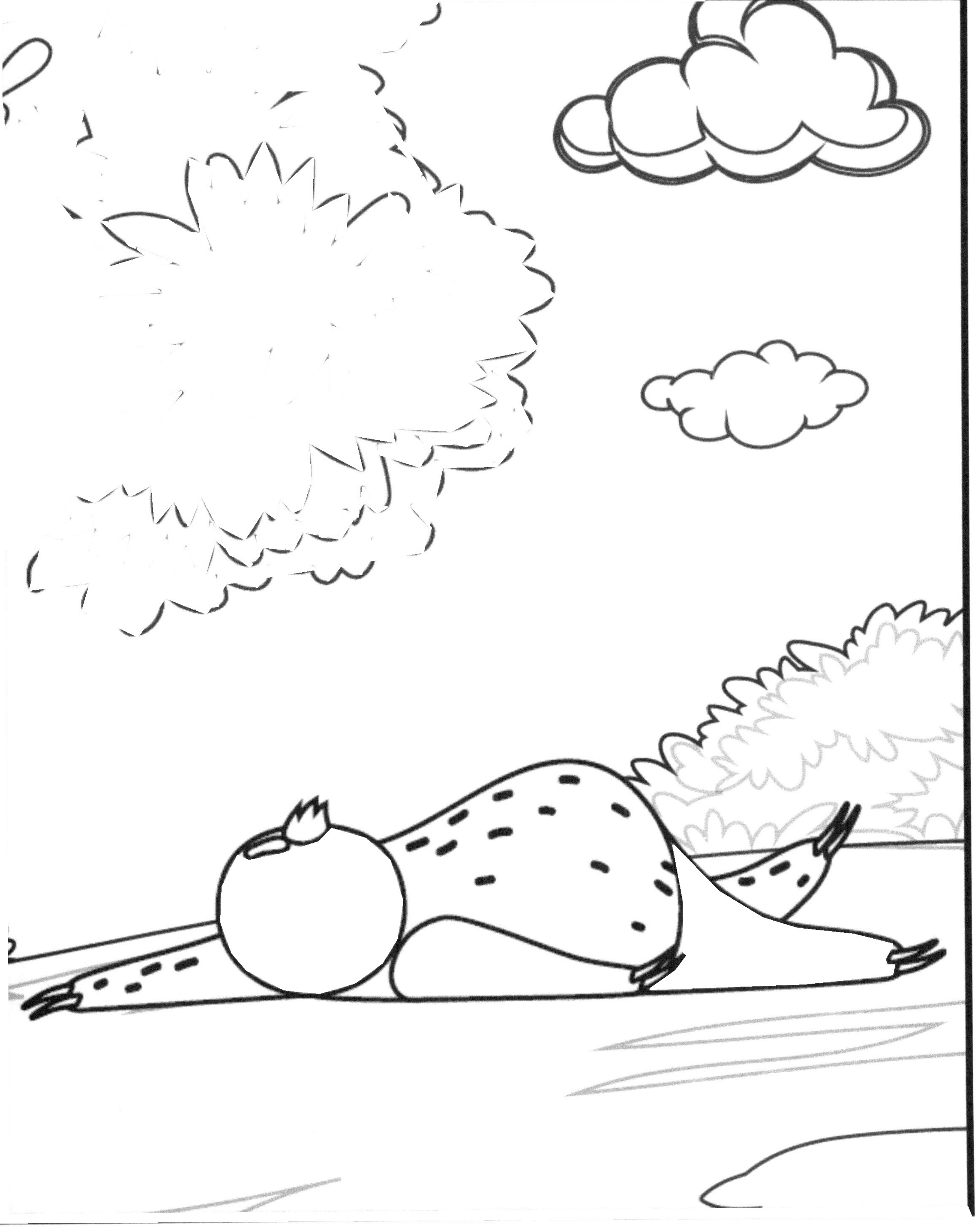

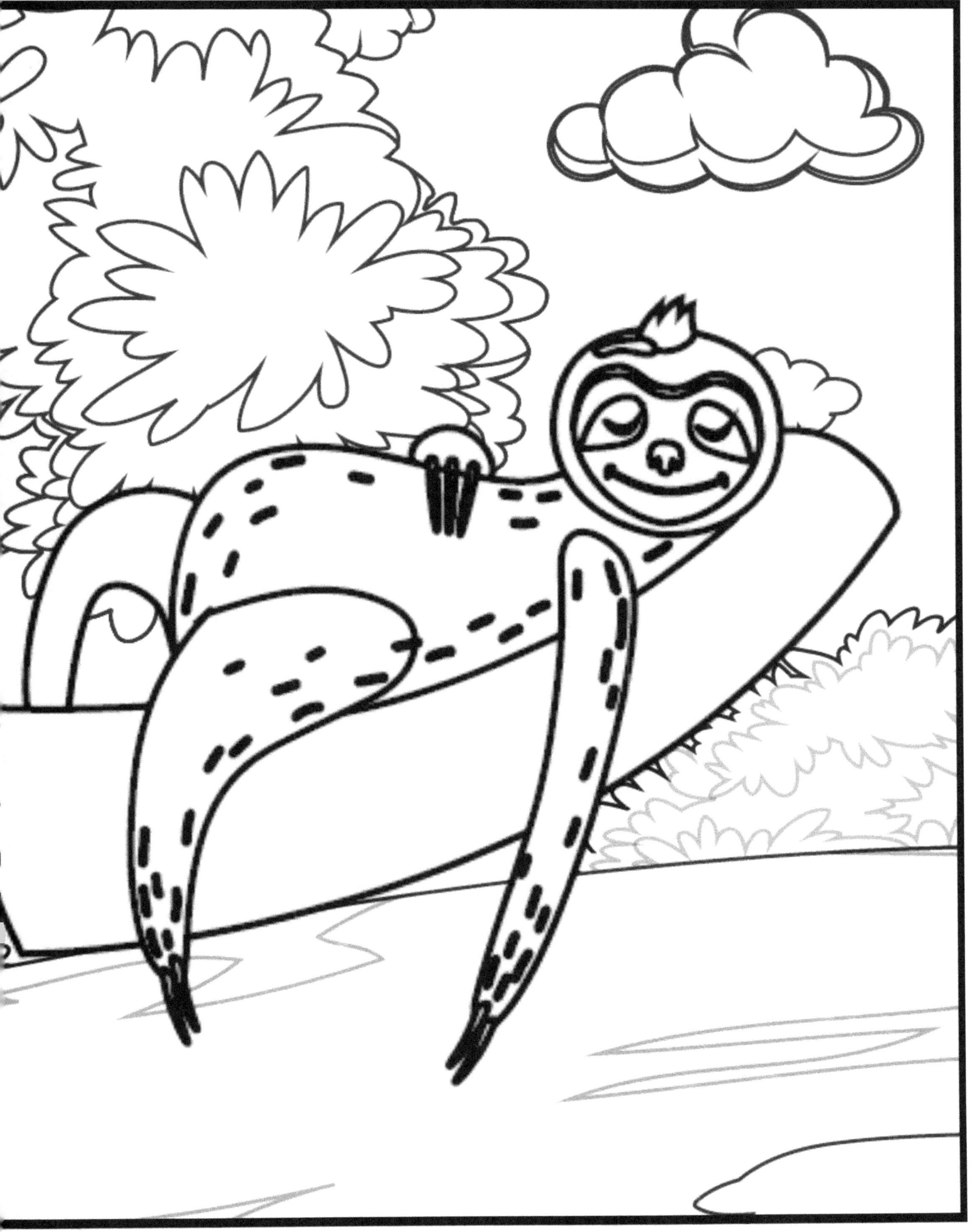

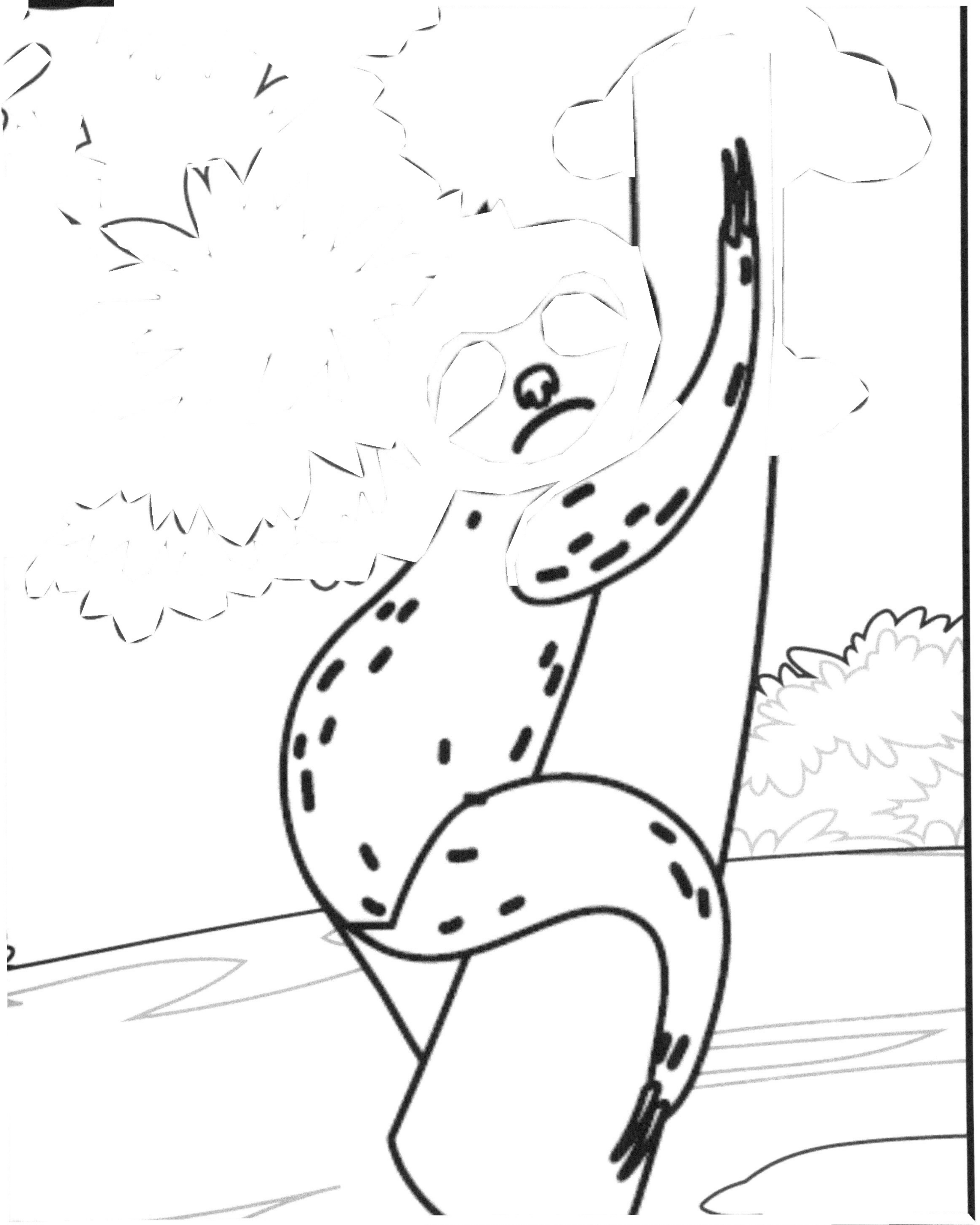

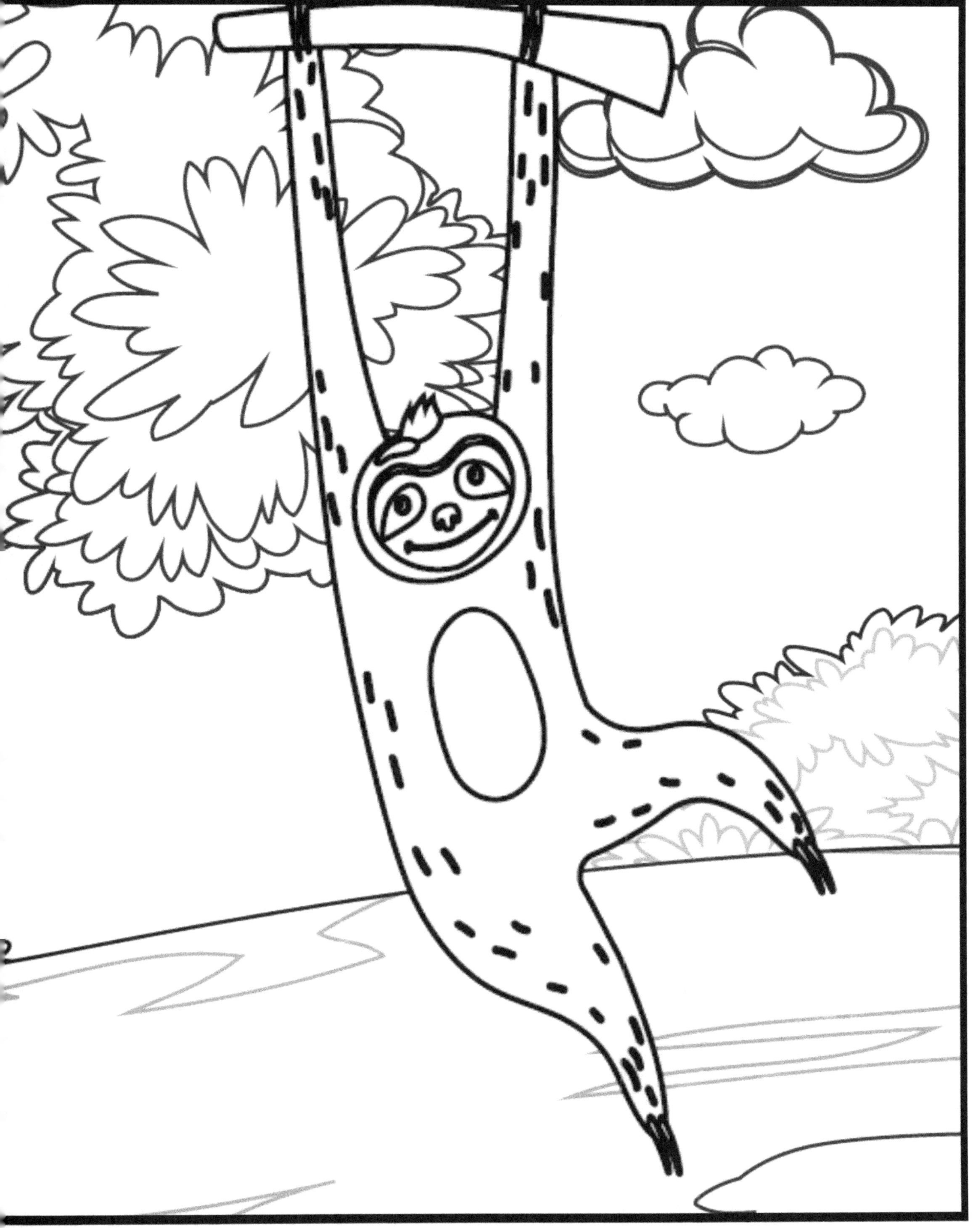

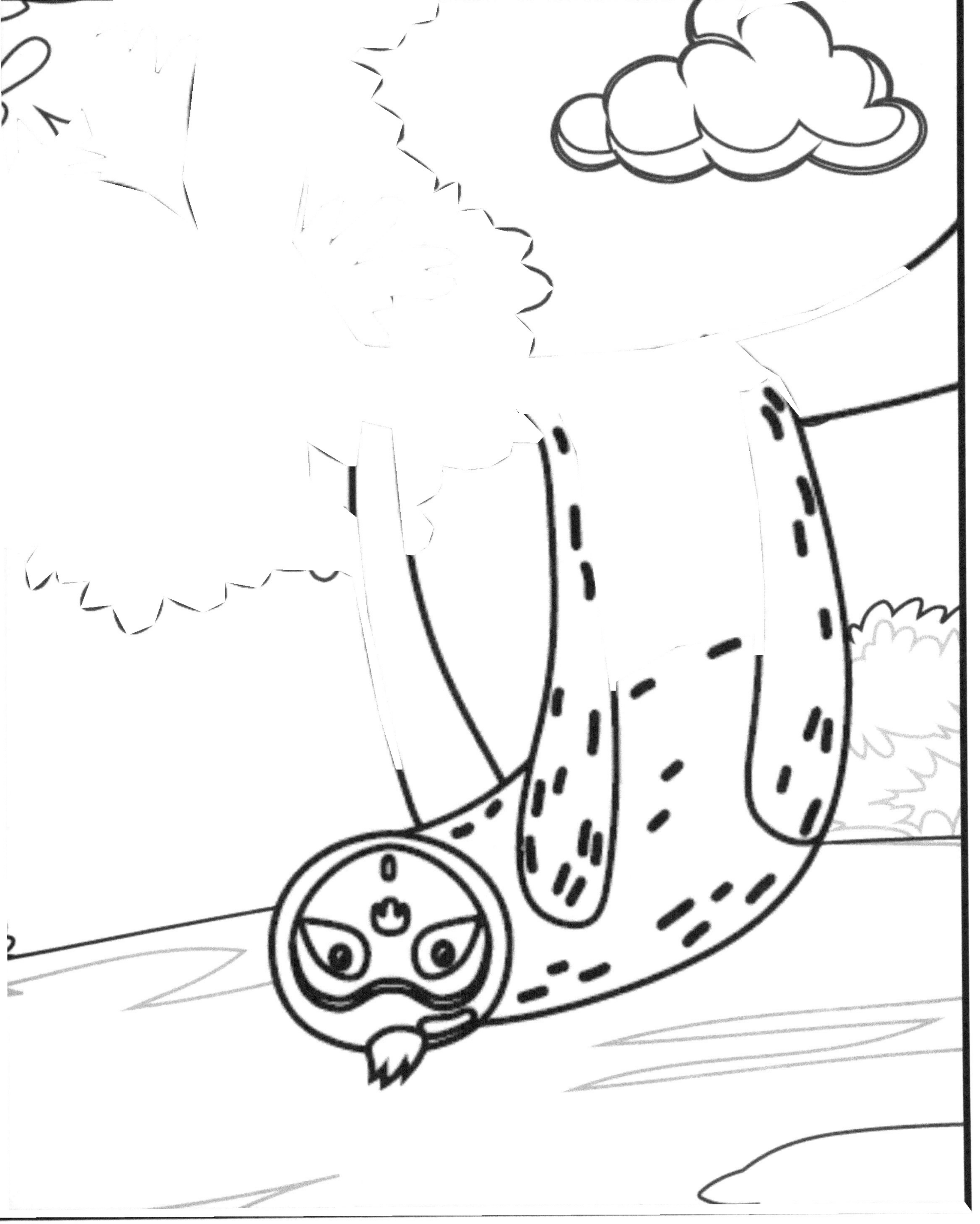

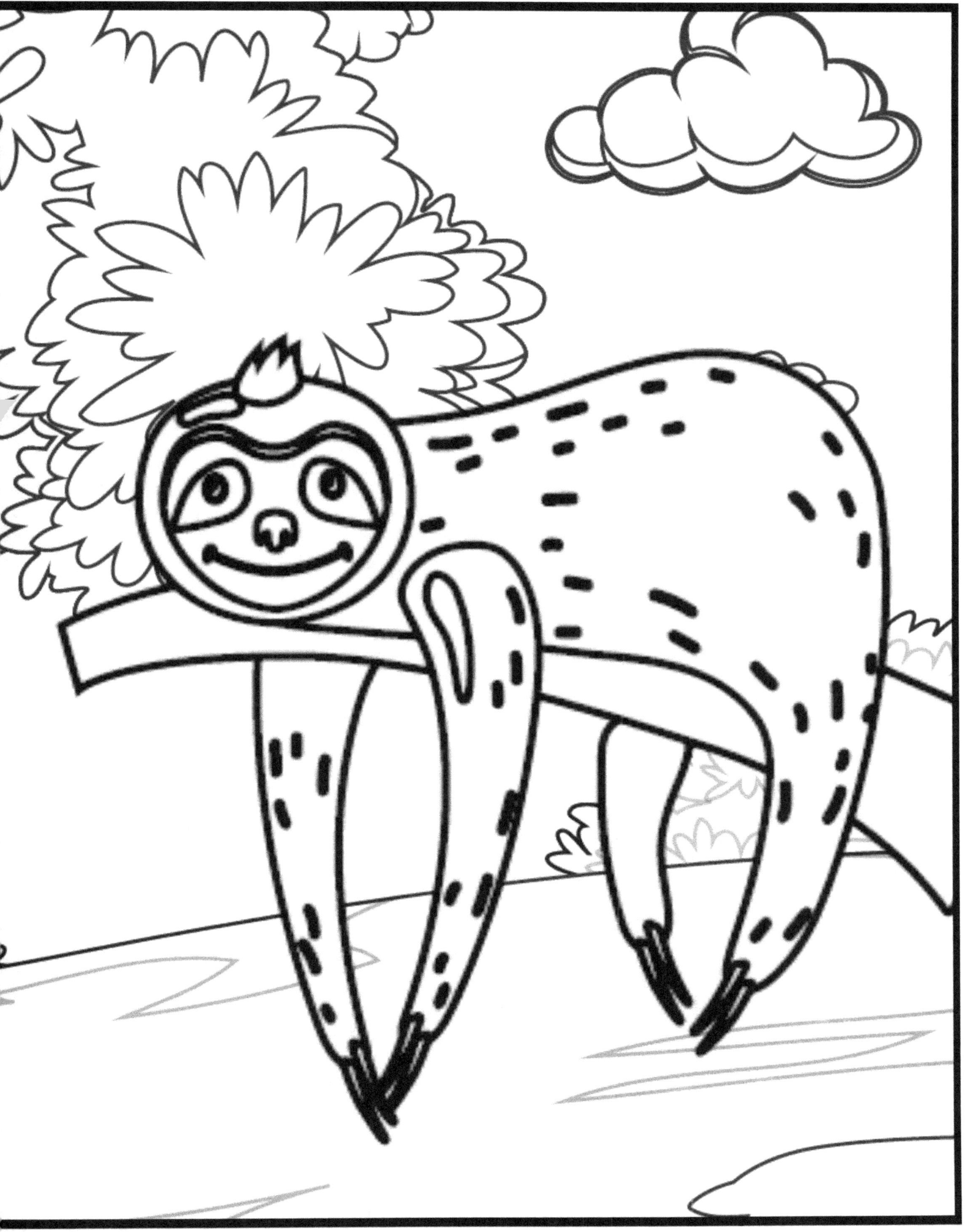

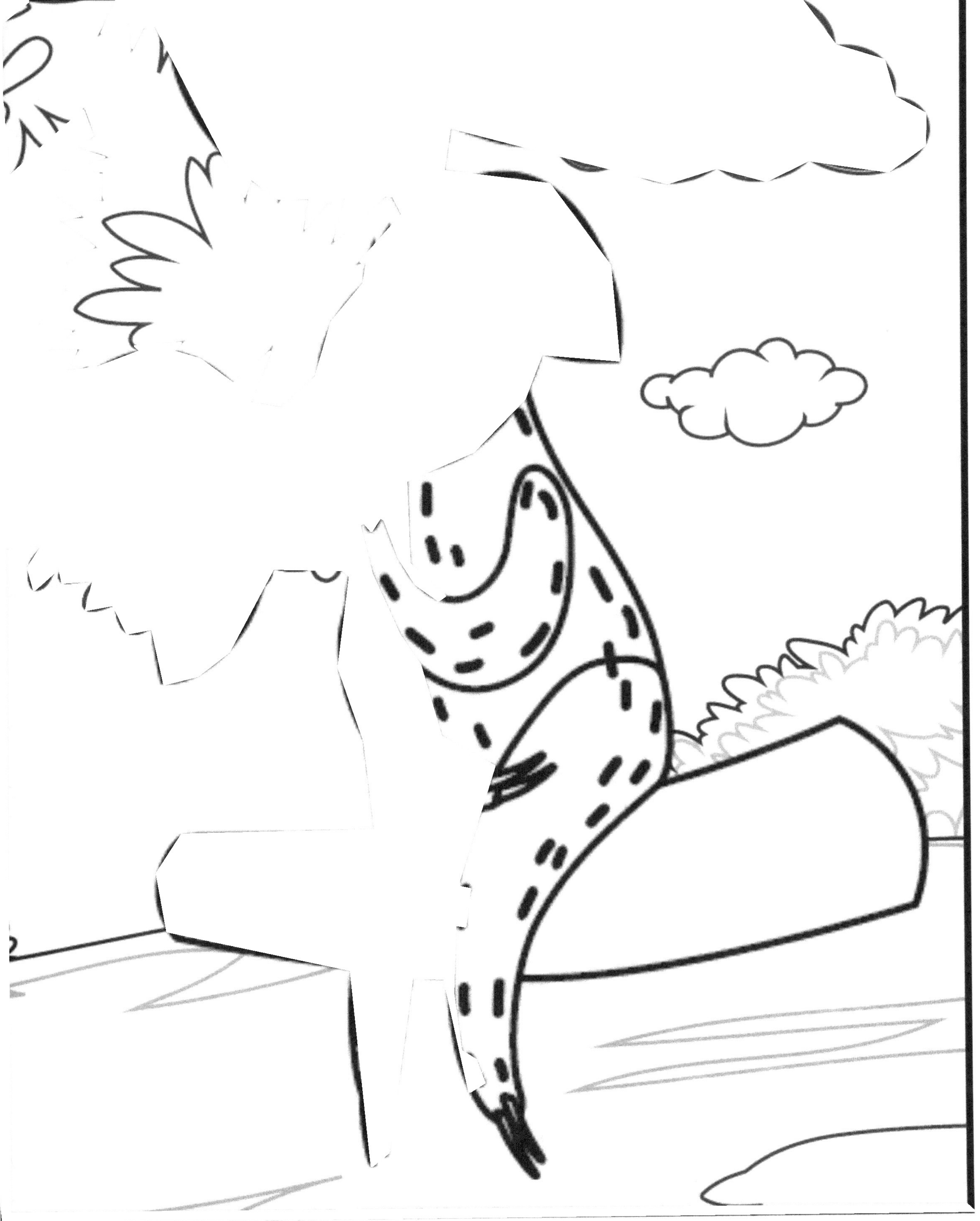

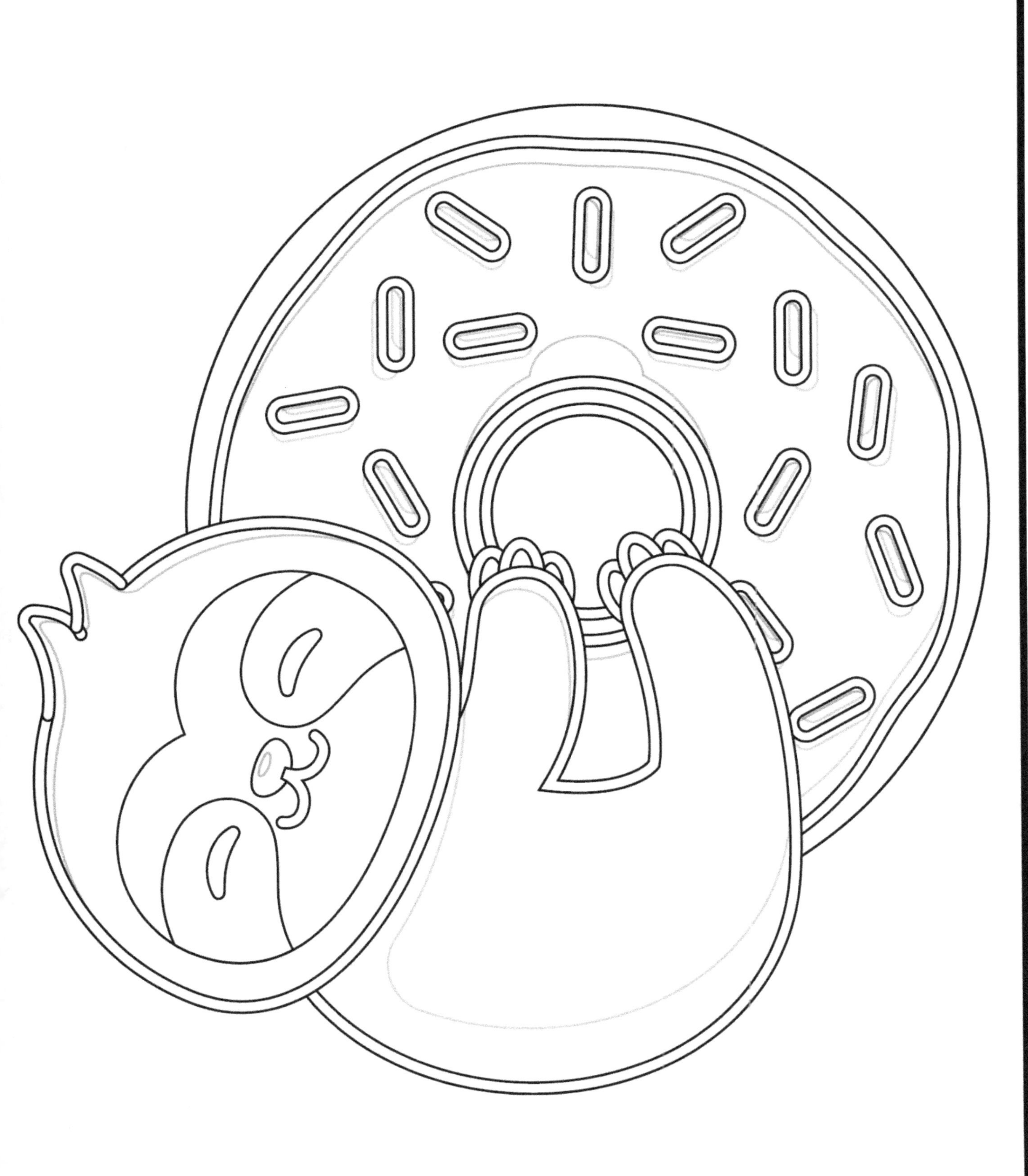